BATTLE OF THE FLESH VS. THE SPIRIT:
A STUDY OF THE LIFE OF JACOB

Retreat Leader Guide
WORKBOOK
RICHARD T. CASE

Acknowledgments

I wish to dedicate this course to and thank all of the leaders of our **Ministry: All For Jesus—ABIDE Ministries** along with my wife. Linda, who have all walked together with us as we receive and live out the life of the Spirit, knowing we have a battle with the flesh. These leaders faithfully have consistently shared the constant struggle with this battle; and walked together into the victory of life in the Spirit in each of our personal lives. Then they all have been teaching their groups and friends how to understand this battle and walked with them to then also live out the victory of life in the Spirit. Most importantly, they all know that living in the flesh is not to be accepted as normal, but rather living in the Spirit is to be normal, and as we then do struggle with the flesh. we experience the awareness of this, now the remedy of immediate return to the Kingdom and life of God. and thus live normally in the fullness of the Spirit, as intended. This course presents such important truths and we are blessed that we all. especially Linda. have fully embraced this and are being blessed as they give it away—and literally hundreds of others are now receiving it and giving it away. Overcoming this battle is so important to the church universal—God's way of us living with Him to receive the superabundant life—Thank you all:

These leaders are:
Jake & Mary Beckel
Joe & Leigh Bogar
Rich & Janet Cocchiaro
Larry & Sherry Collet
Scott & Kristen Cornell
David & Melissa Dunkel
Tom & Susanne Ewing
Rick & Kelly Ferris
Joel & Christina Gunn
Scott & Terry Hitchcock
Rick & Nancy Hoover
Tad & Monica Jones
Ed & Becky Kobel
Don & Rachelle Light
Chris & Heidi May
Terry & Josephine Noetzel
Towanda Norton
Steve & Carolyn Van Ooteghem
Preston & Lynda Pitts
Dan & Kathy Rocconi
Bob & Keri Rockwell
John & Michelle Santaferraro
Allyson & Denny Weinberg
Neal & Kathy Weisenburger

Further, it is a joy for me to share this life with my wife. Linda. and family who together are enjoying the fruits of overcoming this battle. What an honor and a privilege for us.

BATTLE OF THE FLESH VS THE SPIRIT: A STUDY OF THE LIFE OF JACOB
PUBLISHED BY LIVING WATERS—ABIDE MINISTRIES
7615 Lemon Gulch Way
Castle Rock, CO 80108

Unless otherwise noted, all Scripture quotations are from the ESV® Bible (The Holy Bible, English Standard Version®), copyright © 2001 by Crossway Bibles, a publishing ministry of Good News Publishers. Used by permission. All rights reserved.

ISBN: 979-8-21811533-3
Copyright © 2024 by Richard T. Case.

All rights reserved. No part of this publication may be reproduced, distributed or transmitted in any form or by any means, including photocopying, recording, or other electronic or mechanical methods, without the prior written permission of the publisher.

Publisher's Cataloging-in-Publication data

Names:
Title:
Description: .
Identifiers: ISBN | LCCN
Subjects:

Printed in the United States of America 2024 — 2nd ed

TABLE OF CONTENTS

Lesson One:
Cause of the Battle of the Flesh & Consequences; Covenant For Abraham For Believers—
Struggle of the Flesh 2

Lesson Two:
Difference Between Esau (Representing Life in the Flesh)
And Jacob (Representing Life in the Spirit) 22

Lesson Three:
Jacob's Battle of the Flesh, Experience of Victory Over the Flesh,
God's Faithfulness Despite the Flesh 38

Lesson Four:
Jacob's Wrestling With God As He Understands Surrender;
Israel's Continued Battle With the Flesh/ the Enemy (Esau's Descendants). 54

Lesson Five:
How We Life in the Spirit And Experience God's Power Over the Flesh And the Enemy 72

LESSON 1:
CAUSE OF THE BATTLE OF THE FLESH & CONSEQUENCES; COVENANT FOR ABRAHAM FOR BELIEVERS—STRUGGLE OF THE FLESH

Welcome to our course: *The Battle of the Flesh Versus the Spirit*, as seen through a study of the life of Jacob. This study will help explain how this battle applies to us. Paul stated in Romans specifically that this is a real battle and again in Galatians, where he tells believers there's a fight between the Spirit and the flesh. As believers, remember, we aren't automatically put in a place of following the Holy Spirit or being led by the Holy Spirit. Instead, there is a battle; and the battle is going to wind up being the choices we make and the heart desire that we have.

In this study, we will dig deeper into what this means. What does it mean to be in the flesh? What are the implications of being in the flesh? What does it mean to follow the Spirit? Through Jacob's life, we will work toward understanding what it means to walk—and even wrestle with—God. We invite you to this course first to receive the truth and then to experience the victory that's going to come from living in the Spirit and not the flesh.

As we begin, we first have to address an issue that is basic in life: the flesh. It's called the sinful nature. Most believers realize they have a sinful nature, thinking "Isn't that normal, and aren't I basically going to fail even though I'm trying to be a solid Christian?" Paul describes this battle in a much deeper and more pure way.

> "Most believers realize they have a sinful nature, thinking "Isn't that normal, and aren't I basically going to fail even though I'm trying to be a solid Christian?"

Read through these verses and write out the description of the battle of the flesh. What is the outcome of this battle for how we live out our lives? Why?

Read Romans 7:18-23: 18

^{18}For I know that nothing good dwells in me, that is, in my flesh. For I have the desire to do what is right, but not the ability to carry it out. ^{19} For I do not do the good I want, but the evil I do not want is what I keep on doing. ^{20} Now if I do what I do not want, it is no longer I who do it, but sin that dwells within me.

^{21} So I find it to be a law that when I want to do right, evil lies close at hand. ^{22} For I delight in the law of God, in my inner being, ^{23} but I see in my members another law waging war against the law of my mind and making me captive to the law of sin that dwells in my members.

LESSON 1:
CAUSE OF THE BATTLE OF THE FLESH & CONSEQUENCES; COVENANT FOR ABRAHAM FOR BELIEVERS—STRUGGLE OF THE FLESH

_____
_____
_____
_____
_____

Paul says, "My desire is to live the life of God. However, I have a problem." What's the problem? "Flesh. Regardless of my desire, I'd like to follow God. I'd like to follow the scriptures. I'd like to do the things that God says, but I fail." Then, he says, "I find something interesting. A law. What that means is that it's universal. It's not only you who tries and fails, but everyone as we are all covered by one universal truth and that is no matter how hard we try, we all battle the flesh, and oftentimes fail in the battle.

Read through these verses and write out what you see as both the conflict and the consequences if we continue to operate in the flesh (self).

> **Read Galatians 5:17:**
>
> ¹⁷ For the desires of the flesh are against the Spirit, and the desires of the Spirit are against the flesh, for these are opposed to each other, to keep you from doing the things you want to do.

_____
_____
_____
_____
_____

The desire of the flesh is against the desires of the Spirit and the desire of the Spirit is against the desires of the flesh. They oppose each other. Which implies what? A conflict. You have a problem, and it's resident within you. But you aren't alone in this. It is universal for all believers.

LESSON 1:
CAUSE OF THE BATTLE OF THE FLESH & CONSEQUENCES; COVENANT FOR ABRAHAM FOR BELIEVERS—STRUGGLE OF THE FLESH

> **Read Romans 8:5–8:**
>
> ⁵ For those who live according to the flesh set their minds on the things of the flesh, but those who live according to the Spirit set their minds on the things of the Spirit. ⁶ For to set the mind on the flesh is death, but to set the mind on the Spirit is life and peace. ⁷ For the mind that is set on the flesh is hostile to God, for it does not submit to God's law; indeed, it cannot. ⁸ Those who are in the flesh cannot please God.

_____
_____
_____
_____
_____

If you set your mind on the flesh (remember the definition here, your self-will, deciding on your own what you want to do), including, as Paul described it as actually trying to do good things, but doing so in your own self-will (I will, I should), he says: There is a problem. You're in the flesh, not the Spirit. The consequences to the believer are threefold in this verse:

1. You put to death the life of the Spirit. You're back to Adam and Eve, where they fell and they lost that communion with God. So, you are putting to death the Spirit as if it doesn't exist—negating the power and life of the Spirit.

2. You become hostile to God, have enmity against God, or work against God. This is intriguing. You're trying to please God, but because you're doing it in the flesh, what are you doing? You're not allowing Him to do the work to bring you victory over what you're trying to overcome. You're working against Him and moving deeper away from Him, and He can't resolve it. Why? Because you're at enmity against Him, so you are working against Him and He against you.

3. You cannot please Him. You can't please Him because He can't deliver to you the beautiful life of the Spirit. The real battle is that you are trying to gain all of this on your own.

LESSON 1:
CAUSE OF THE BATTLE OF THE FLESH & CONSEQUENCES; COVENANT FOR ABRAHAM FOR BELIEVERS—STRUGGLE OF THE FLESH

We all have a fundamental problem, and that is our sin nature. We're born with it. We live with it. When you become a believer, does your sin nature become perfected? No, you still have it. It's called the flesh, the self, the carnal. Does it get any better? No, your flesh doesn't get any better. Paul says according to the law of the flesh/self (truth of the sin nature), this is our default position of how we operate in life. It is self and the flesh. It's not a neutral thing. Our desire is to please God, but since we are living in the flesh, and don't walk in the Spirit, this is impossible. If we don't walk in the Spirit, our default is back to the flesh, and we're at enmity against God. This is the critical issue of our spiritual life.

We know that unbelievers do not have the Spirit and by definition, live in the flesh, the carnal, and are self-centered. They have thus put to death the Spirit (it is not resident with them), are at enmity against God, and cannot please God.

For believers we still have the potential to be operating as practical unbelievers, but many of us do not understand this potential. As believers, we think that because we believe, everything that happens to us (including our struggles with things we know are not pleasing to God) is God's will. After all, isn't God in control, and isn't He good? However, there's another demarcation to believers. Paul calls it carnal, where you are living in self. Why? Because you're not being led by the Spirit. So, by definition, you're a self-centered, carnal believer. And the consequences are that you're actually working against God, and your life is a struggle, even though you have good intentions. You would like to get better. You'd like to overcome this addiction. You'd like to stop being angry. You'd like to be more kind. But God says: You can't fully get there in the carnal, so your only solution is to be led by the Spirit. In the Spirit, we are doing the work and fulfilling our life through God. We are living as intended and are the visual representation of the invisible God. We want to live our life through Him, Christ in us, the hope of glory.

Note, then, that we have three segmentations: unbeliever, carnal believer (yes, they're going to be eternally with God, which is good news. See 1 Corinthians 3 for Paul's statement of this—those who live in the carnal can have the activity of their lives burned up as worthless hay, but they get to be with God in heaven. That's good if you truly made that transaction); and spirit–led believer, who is living the life of God. Thus, every believer then has the battle of the Spirit versus the flesh. And it's truly a battle that lasts your whole life and always ends up being an issue. That's why this course is so critical. The battle never ends. And it's one that we must constantly deal with, day by day by day.

LESSON 1:
CAUSE OF THE BATTLE OF THE FLESH & CONSEQUENCES; COVENANT FOR ABRAHAM FOR BELIEVERS—STRUGGLE OF THE FLESH

Read through these verses and write out what the Covenant is and what the primary benefits of the Covenant are to us.

THE COVENANT:

> **Read Genesis 12:1–3:**
>
> The Call of Abram
> **12** Now the Lord said[a] to Abram, "Go from your country[b] and your kindred and your father's house to the land that I will show you. ² And I will make of you a great nation, and I will bless you and make your name great, so that you will be a blessing. ³ I will bless those who bless you, and him who dishonors you I will curse, and in you all the families of the earth shall be blessed."[c]

_____
_____
_____
_____
_____

God said, "Through your walk with Me, I'm going to bless you to make you a blessing. It's called the Covenant. I'm establishing the Covenant and through you, all the families of Earth can live in this Covenant. It's going to happen through you." By definition, what does that imply? He's going to have what? Children. He's going to have offspring because it's going to start through you, and it'll be extended through you.

> **Read Genesis 17:1–10:**
>
> Abraham and the Covenant of Circumcision
> **17** When Abram was ninety-nine years old the Lord appeared to Abram and said to him, "I am God Almighty;[a] walk before me, and be blameless, ² that I may make my covenant between me and you, and may multiply you greatly." ³ Then Abram fell on his face. And God said to him, ⁴ "Behold, my covenant is with you, and you shall be the father of a multitude of nations. ⁵ No longer shall your name be called Abram,[b] but your name shall be Abraham,[c] for I have made you the father of a multitude of nations. ⁶ I will make you exceedingly fruitful, and I

LESSON 1:
CAUSE OF THE BATTLE OF THE FLESH & CONSEQUENCES; COVENANT FOR ABRAHAM FOR BELIEVERS—STRUGGLE OF THE FLESH

> will make you into nations, and kings shall come from you. 7 And I will establish my covenant between me and you and your offspring after you throughout their generations for an everlasting covenant, to be God to you and to your offspring after you. 8 And I will give to you and to your offspring after you the land of your sojournings, all the land of Canaan, for an everlasting possession, and I will be their God."
>
> 9 And God said to Abraham, "As for you, you shall keep my covenant, you and your offspring after you throughout their generations. 10 This is my covenant, which you shall keep, between me and you and your offspring after you: Every male among you shall be circumcised.

_____
_____
_____
_____
_____

He lays out the Covenant, "Here's what I'm going to do. You're going to have offspring and all of your offspring will be recipients of the Covenant, which lasts forever. It's going to come through you if you walk with Me; you'll be blessed to be a blessing and the Covenant will follow generation by generation by generation. You will experience the Covenant as I am giving to you. And remember, the Covenant is simple."

What does God say? He's going to make you a blessing. He's going to bless you so that you will bless others. It's a flow-through process. This is valid for all believers. Paul describes this in Galatians.

Read through these verses and write out who the recipient of the Covenant really is. Why is that important to us as believers?

> **Read Galatians 3:15–20:**
>
> The Law and the Promise
> 15 To give a human example, brothers:[a] even with a man-made covenant, no one annuls it or adds to it once it has been ratified. 16 Now the promises were made to Abraham and to his offspring. It does not say, "And to offsprings,"

LESSON 1:
CAUSE OF THE BATTLE OF THE FLESH & CONSEQUENCES; COVENANT FOR ABRAHAM FOR BELIEVERS—STRUGGLE OF THE FLESH

> referring to many, but referring to one, "And to your offspring," who is Christ. [17] This is what I mean: the law, which came 430 years afterward, does not annul a covenant previously ratified by God, so as to make the promise void. [18] For if the inheritance comes by the law, it no longer comes by promise; but God gave it to Abraham by a promise.
>
> [19] Why then the law? It was added because of transgressions, until the offspring should come to whom the promise had been made, and it was put in place through angels by an intermediary. [20] Now an intermediary implies more than one, but God is one.

_____
_____
_____
_____
_____

He gave the promise to Abraham, "I will bless you to make you a blessing." But, He says the Covenant is not to seeds (plural), meaning all of Abraham's offspring (including us as believers), but to His seed (singular), who is Christ.

Who then is the recipient of the Covenant? Christ. He's the only one.

In order for us to receive it, what must we be in? We must be in Him, walking with Him. Just because you're part of God's family does not mean that your guaranteed to receive the Covenant. In the Old Testament, a member of the nation of Israel (a Jew who is Abraham's offspring) did not automatically experience the fullness of the Covenant. Each person had to perform the requirements of the Covenant and walk with God individually. In Jeremiah's time, the nation of Israel fell away through operating in the flesh, and were judged, destroyed by Nebuchadnezzar, not receiving the Covenant. The only ones who received the Covenant when Israel was judged and taken over by Nebuchadnezzar and carried off to Babylon were the remnant. Which illustrates the essence of the life of believers with God—a choice to participate in the Covenant through following Him, or not participating in the Covenant through living in self, apart from the relationship with God. And living in the Covenant is not

LESSON 1:
CAUSE OF THE BATTLE OF THE FLESH & CONSEQUENCES; COVENANT FOR ABRAHAM FOR BELIEVERS—STRUGGLE OF THE FLESH

dependent upon our circumstances. In the case of the remnant, they received the Covenant even though they lost their homeland and all the normal living there—life was still grand in a difficult and foreign place. Life was different, but the remnant (those who follow and live in God, in the Spirit) still received the Covenant—blessed to be a blessing.

For those of us now living in New Testament times, we understand that the Covenant has been given to Christ. He will deliver it you when you are walking with Him, as is the spirit of receiving the Covenant. Christ, alone, is the recipient of the Covenant, and then He gives it to all who walk with Him and receive it from Him. Not because we are seeds (believers) but only because we are IN HIM.

Read through these verses and write out what happened when Abraham and Sarah acted in the flesh (self). Why did they act this way, and what was the consequence? Why is that important to us?

> **Read Genesis 20:1–10:**
>
> **Abraham and Abimelech**
> **20** From there Abraham journeyed toward the territory of the Negeb and lived between Kadesh and Shur; and he sojourned in Gerar. ² And Abraham said of Sarah his wife, "She is my sister." And Abimelech king of Gerar sent and took Sarah. ³ But God came to Abimelech in a dream by night and said to him, "Behold, you are a dead man because of the woman whom you have taken, for she is a man's wife." ⁴ Now Abimelech had not approached her. So he said, "Lord, will you kill an innocent people? ⁵ Did he not himself say to me, 'She is my sister'? And she herself said, 'He is my brother.' In the integrity of my heart and the innocence of my hands I have done this." ⁶ Then God said to him in the dream, "Yes, I know that you have done this in the integrity of your heart, and it was I who kept you from sinning against me. Therefore, I did not let you touch her. ⁷ Now then, return the man's wife, for he is a prophet, so that he will pray for you, and you shall live. But if you do not return her, know that you shall surely die, you and all who are yours."
>
> ⁸ So Abimelech rose early in the morning and called all his servants and told them all these things. And the men were very much afraid. ⁹ Then Abimelech called Abraham and said to him, "What have you done to us? And how have I sinned against you, that you have brought on me and my kingdom a great sin? You have done to me things that ought not to be done." ¹⁰ And Abimelech said to Abraham, "What did you see, that you did this thing?"

LESSON 1:
CAUSE OF THE BATTLE OF THE FLESH & CONSEQUENCES; COVENANT FOR ABRAHAM FOR BELIEVERS—STRUGGLE OF THE FLESH

_____

_____

_____

_____

_____

Here we see a problem. Abraham understood His promise, the Covenant from God—that he and Sarah were to have a son. But it wasn't happening. Sarah was going through menopause, and Abraham was getting older as well and not capable of having a baby in the natural. What did they conclude? That the promise wasn't going to happen. So, they take matters into their own hands and decide to assist God in delivering this promise. Sarah said to Abraham: Go ahead and lay with Hagar and have a son. This, they do. They have Ishmael. Lots and lots of interesting things here. They have the son. As far as they're concerned, they've created the son of promise. God, afterwards, comes along and says that's not the son of promise. That's not His desire, His promised offspring for them. They did this in the flesh. They decided in the flesh to fulfill something that He had intended to give to them. See how subtle this is? It is as simple as: I heard God's promise, let me go help Him out (this is the very definition of the flesh). So, they have Ishmael, and God said, "That's not him. I'm still going to give you your son, the son of promise." Abraham responds by saying, "Why don't you just take him? It's going to be a lot easier. Why don't you just take him and name him the son the promise? I mean, come on, he's already here." God says, "No, absolutely not, he's not the son of promise." Abraham and Sarah believed Him and continued to follow and live in God. They then have a baby named Isaac. Miraculously, the son of promise. So now, they have both, the son of flesh and the son of promise. What did God tell him to do? Cast out the son of the flesh. Cast out the bondwoman and her son. Paul, who's a student of the Old Testament because he was the Pharisee of the Pharisees, gives us deeper understanding of this as it relates to our life.

Read through these verses and write out what we are to do regarding our flesh (self). What choice do we have, and why is this so important to choose rightly?

> **Read Galatians 4:21–31:**
>
> Example of Hagar and Sarah
> [21] Tell me, you who desire to be under the law, do you not listen to the law? [22] For it is written that Abraham had two sons, one by a slave woman

LESSON 1:
CAUSE OF THE BATTLE OF THE FLESH & CONSEQUENCES; COVENANT FOR ABRAHAM FOR BELIEVERS—STRUGGLE OF THE FLESH

> and one by a free woman. 23 But the son of the slave was born according to the flesh, while the son of the free woman was born through promise. 24 Now this may be interpreted allegorically: these women are two covenants. One is from Mount Sinai, bearing children for slavery; she is Hagar. 25 Now Hagar is Mount Sinai in Arabia;[a] she corresponds to the present Jerusalem, for she is in slavery with her children. 26 But the Jerusalem above is free, and she is our mother. 27 For it is written,
>
> "Rejoice, O barren one who does not bear;
>   break forth and cry aloud, you who are not in labor!
> For the children of the desolate one will be more
>   than those of the one who has a husband."
>
> 28 Now you,[b] brothers, like Isaac, are children of promise. 29 But just as at that time he who was born according to the flesh persecuted him who was born according to the Spirit, so also it is now. 30 But what does the Scripture say? "Cast out the slave woman and her son, for the son of the slave woman shall not inherit with the son of the free woman." 31 So, brothers, we are not children of the slave but of the free woman.

_____
_____
_____
_____
_____

    So, He says: Hagar and Ismael were of the flesh, the bondwoman and her son. Isaac, though, is the son of the Covenant, the promise, the son of the freewoman. God tells Abraham that he must cast out the bondwoman and her son, who are of the flesh, and instead live in the Spirit. But it's his choice. He says to Abraham, "Are you going to decide on your own what is a good idea? Or are you going to follow Me? You're going to have to make a choice."

LESSON 1:
CAUSE OF THE BATTLE OF THE FLESH & CONSEQUENCES; COVENANT FOR ABRAHAM FOR BELIEVERS—STRUGGLE OF THE FLESH

Read through these verses and write out the choices that are set before us. What is important to choose rightly? Why is this so critical to our walk with God and experiencing the Covenant?

> **Read Deuteronomy 30:11–20:**
>
> The Choice of Life and Death
> [11] "For this commandment that I command you today is not too hard for you, neither is it far off. [12] It is not in heaven, that you should say, 'Who will ascend to heaven for us and bring it to us, that we may hear it and do it?' [13] Neither is it beyond the sea, that you should say, 'Who will go over the sea for us and bring it to us, that we may hear it and do it?' [14] But the word is very near you. It is in your mouth and in your heart, so that you can do it.
>
> [15] "See, I have set before you today life and good, death and evil. [16] If you obey the commandments of the Lord your God[a] that I command you today, by loving the Lord your God, by walking in his ways, and by keeping his commandments and his statutes and his rules,[b] then you shall live and multiply, and the Lord your God will bless you in the land that you are entering to take possession of it. [17] But if your heart turns away, and you will not hear, but are drawn away to worship other gods and serve them, [18] I declare to you today, that you shall surely perish. You shall not live long in the land that you are going over the Jordan to enter and possess. [19] I call heaven and earth to witness against you today, that I have set before you life and death, blessing and curse. Therefore, choose life, that you and your offspring may live, [20] loving the Lord your God, obeying his voice and holding fast to him, for he is your life and length of days, that you may dwell in the land that the Lord swore to your fathers, to Abraham, to Isaac, and to Jacob, to give them."

_____
_____
_____
_____

LESSON 1:
CAUSE OF THE BATTLE OF THE FLESH & CONSEQUENCES; COVENANT FOR ABRAHAM FOR BELIEVERS—STRUGGLE OF THE FLESH

The process of following God and living in Him is not that difficult. You don't need somebody else to go get it for you. You don't need a pastor to help you. You don't need somebody else. This is actually quite simple and is offered to everyone. Do you want what He sets before you? Life or death. Blessing or cursing. He defines it. Choosing life is choosing Him, walking in the Spirit, letting Him guide you, lead you, deliver to you, fulfill His promises to you. Let Him fulfill His promises to you, and you cling to Him. He's going to do the work because it's going to be a spiritual process.

Of course, you can choose the opposite. You can choose your own will, the flesh. You don't have to choose God. By default, if you do not actively choose God, you automatically choose the flesh—and it is not going to be pleasant. You're going to have consequences. God set before you life or death, blessing or cursing. Jesus reiterates this when He says, "Daily, deny self, take up your cross, and follow Me. The life is in following Him; and we have to choose this. The life of God comes through the choice of following God. And now it's resident in Christ. And of course, Christ is in us. So, our role is simply to learn to follow Christ. We find the depth of this through the life of Jacob, and what it means to live in the flesh or the Spirit, particularly when it comes to wrestling with God.

Let's go into the life of Jacob now and see how this applies to us.

Read through these verses and write out the description of each character: Jacob and Esau. What do each represent? What strikes you about what happened as it relates to how we respond to God?

> **Read Genesis 25:7–28:**
>
> [7] These are the days of the years of Abraham's life, 175 years. [8] Abraham breathed his last and died in a good old age, an old man and full of years, and was gathered to his people. [9] Isaac and Ishmael his sons buried him in the cave of Machpelah, in the field of Ephron the son of Zohar the Hittite, east of Mamre, [10] the field that Abraham purchased from the Hittites. There Abraham was buried, with Sarah his wife. [11] After the death of Abraham, God blessed Isaac his son. And Isaac settled at Beer-lahai-roi.
>
> [12] These are the generations of Ishmael, Abraham's son, whom Hagar the Egyptian, Sarah's servant, bore to Abraham. [13] These are the names of the sons of Ishmael, named in the order of their birth: Nebaioth, the firstborn of Ishmael; and Kedar, Adbeel, Mibsam, [14] Mishma, Dumah, Massa, [15] Hadad, Tema, Jetur, Naphish, and Kedemah. [16] These are the

LESSON 1:
CAUSE OF THE BATTLE OF THE FLESH & CONSEQUENCES; COVENANT FOR ABRAHAM FOR BELIEVERS—STRUGGLE OF THE FLESH

sons of Ishmael and these are their names, by their villages and by their encampments, twelve princes according to their tribes. 17 (These are the years of the life of Ishmael: 137 years. He breathed his last and died, and was gathered to his people.) 18 They settled from Havilah to Shur, which is opposite Egypt in the direction of Assyria. He settled[a] over against all his kinsmen.

The Birth of Esau and Jacob

19 These are the generations of Isaac, Abraham's son: Abraham fathered Isaac, 20 and Isaac was forty years old when he took Rebekah, the daughter of Bethuel the Aramean of Paddan-aram, the sister of Laban the Aramean, to be his wife. 21 And Isaac prayed to the Lord for his wife, because she was barren. And the Lord granted his prayer, and Rebekah his wife conceived. 22 The children struggled together within her, and she said, "If it is thus, why is this happening to me?"[b] So she went to inquire of the Lord. 23 And the Lord said to her,

"Two nations are in your womb,
    and two peoples from within you[c] shall be divided;
the one shall be stronger than the other,
    the older shall serve the younger."

24 When her days to give birth were completed, behold, there were twins in her womb. 25 The first came out red, all his body like a hairy cloak, so they called his name Esau. 26 Afterward his brother came out with his hand holding Esau's heel, so his name was called Jacob.[d] Isaac was sixty years old when she bore them.

27 When the boys grew up, Esau was a skillful hunter, a man of the field, while Jacob was a quiet man, dwelling in tents. 28 Isaac loved Esau because he ate of his game, but Rebekah loved Jacob.

_____
_____
_____
_____
_____

LESSON 1:
CAUSE OF THE BATTLE OF THE FLESH & CONSEQUENCES; COVENANT FOR ABRAHAM FOR BELIEVERS—STRUGGLE OF THE FLESH

The structure now from the choice of the flesh and the choice of the Spirit by Abraham and Sarah is in their offspring, Ishmael and Isaac. Ishmael has twelve sons who are the forefathers of the Muslims. As descendants of Ishmael, they look at the twelve tribes as their genealogy, and they today are looking for what's called the twelfth Imam—the one who will bring about the end of the world. Ishmael is the son of the bondwoman, who represents unbelievers (and because of the love of the Lord, anyone, including Muslims, can accept Christ and thus become believers. These believers are called then to choose life and blessing versus living in the flesh.) Isaac (the son of promise) has two sons. Who are they? Esau and Jacob. And they are described as follows:

Esau—hairy, rugged, outdoorsman. He's a hunter who is aggressive and physical.

Jacob—soft-spoken and not as aggressive as Esau.

These two sons will represent the choice we have as believers—life or death, blessing or cursing. Ishmael represents unbelievers. As believers, there is a problem (the issue between Esau and Jacob). Esau represents the flesh, and Jacob represents the Spirit life.

> **Read Genesis 25:29–34:**
>
> Esau Sells His Birthright
> [29] Once when Jacob was cooking stew, Esau came in from the field, and he was exhausted. [30] And Esau said to Jacob, "Let me eat some of that red stew, for I am exhausted!" (Therefore his name was called Edom.[a]) [31] Jacob said, "Sell me your birthright now." [32] Esau said, "I am about to die; of what use is a birthright to me?" [33] Jacob said, "Swear to me now." So he swore to him and sold his birthright to Jacob. [34] Then Jacob gave Esau bread and lentil stew, and he ate and drank and rose and went his way. Thus Esau despised his birthright.

_____

_____

_____

_____

_____

LESSON 1:
CAUSE OF THE BATTLE OF THE FLESH & CONSEQUENCES; COVENANT FOR ABRAHAM FOR BELIEVERS—STRUGGLE OF THE FLESH

We see Esau being driven by desire, the flesh. So, he changes and adds to his name: Edom (we will see the significance of this later). So, Jacob said to Esau who was hungry: Sell me your birthright and Esau agrees, the birthright he believes is nothing, so he can satisfy his life now, the birthright matters not. So, he swore to him and sold his birthright to Jacob. Then Jacob gave Esau bread and lentil stew, and he ate and drank and rose and went his way. It then says Esau despised his birthright. This is very significant.

What's the birthright? The Covenant—the right to receive, especially as the first born, all the inheritance of the father. This includes the essence of the Covenant—blessed to be made a blessing. That was the birthright. It could be received in a similar way by Jacob—he, too, would have inheritance because of the Covenant being given to Abraham's offspring, and their offspring, and their offspring, etc. (Remember, we who are now in the church, as believers are only recipients of the Covenant by choosing to live in Christ who is now the sole recipient of the promise.)

Here, Esau, as the first born (even if only by a few minutes), is the first recipient of the promise, the Covenant, the birthright. What does he do with it? He gives it to Jacob. For what reason? He was hungry.

> **Read again Genesis 25:34:**
>
> ³⁴ Then Jacob gave Esau bread and lentil stew, and he ate and drank and rose and went his way. Thus, Esau despised his birthright.

_____
_____
_____
_____
_____

Esau despised his birthright. Why? It wasn't valuable to him. He didn't think it was worth anything. He was the lawful recipient of the Covenant, but he equated the value of it to a single meal, which is completely temporary. Why? Because he despised it. He knew about it, but he didn't have a heart to follow God. He

LESSON 1:
CAUSE OF THE BATTLE OF THE FLESH & CONSEQUENCES; COVENANT FOR ABRAHAM FOR BELIEVERS—STRUGGLE OF THE FLESH

didn't consider it valuable at all. He said it was worthless. This shows us the deeper spiritual truth. When you're in the flesh, what are you doing? Despising the Covenant. You're despising the Covenant because of what you are saying? It's not that valuable to me because I'm going to do what I want to do as I think I know better (and we will see that this is not a permanent choice, as Jacob also has struggles with the flesh (which, remember, Paul told us was universal, and no believer is exempt from this struggle).

Read through these verses and write out the reason God hated Esau. Since this seems rather harsh and against God's nature, how might we explain this, and what is the significance to us?

> **Read Malachi 1:1–5:**
>
> **1** The oracle of the word of the Lord to Israel by Malachi.[a]
>
> The Lord's Love for Israel
>
> **2** "I have loved you," says the Lord. But you say, "How have you loved us?" "Is not Esau Jacob's brother?" declares the Lord. "Yet I have loved Jacob **3** but Esau I have hated. I have laid waste his hill country and left his heritage to jackals of the desert." **4** If Edom says, "We are shattered but we will rebuild the ruins," the Lord of hosts says, "They may build, but I will tear down, and they will be called 'the wicked country,' and 'the people with whom the Lord is angry forever.'" **5** Your own eyes shall see this, and you shall say, "Great is the Lord beyond the border of Israel!"

_____
_____
_____
_____
_____

    This scripture is difficult to understand. It specifically says that God speaks His perspective toward Esau. Hate. Why? Esau despised receiving the Covenant. As we understand the character of God, could He do anything else? Paul states in Romans 8:5–8 that when we despise following Him by deciding on our own what

LESSON 1:
CAUSE OF THE BATTLE OF THE FLESH & CONSEQUENCES; COVENANT FOR ABRAHAM FOR BELIEVERS—STRUGGLE OF THE FLESH

we want and not pursuing His will or way, we are choosing to set our mind and soul on the flesh, which is what Esau did. It sets up hatred (versus favor), and then we are reminded of the Edomites, the descendants of Esau. They said, "Our life is ruined, but we will rebuild it." We will fix it. And God says what? He will just destroy it again. You will not succeed. You're not going to have the abundant life. You're despising following Him, which Paul writes is the truth of our relationship with Him. It's absolute. God wants us to receive the Covenant, but He can't deliver it to us when we are in the flesh, despising being with Him.

Read through these verses and write out what the difference is between living in the Spirit and living in the flesh. How might we interpret this for our lives today? Why?

Read Obadiah 1:1–16:

¹ The vision of Obadiah.

Edom Will Be Humbled

Thus says the Lord God concerning Edom:
We have heard a report from the Lord,
    and a messenger has been sent among the nations:
"Rise up! Let us rise against her for battle!"
² Behold, I will make you small among the nations;
    you shall be utterly despised.[a]
³ The pride of your heart has deceived you,
    you who live in the clefts of the rock,[b]
    in your lofty dwelling,
who say in your heart,
    "Who will bring me down to the ground?"
⁴ Though you soar aloft like the eagle,
    though your nest is set among the stars,
    from there I will bring you down,
declares the Lord.
⁵ If thieves came to you,
    if plunderers came by night—
    how you have been destroyed!—
    would they not steal only enough for themselves?

LESSON 1:
CAUSE OF THE BATTLE OF THE FLESH & CONSEQUENCES; COVENANT FOR ABRAHAM FOR BELIEVERS—STRUGGLE OF THE FLESH

If grape gatherers came to you,
   would they not leave gleanings?
6 How Esau has been pillaged,
   his treasures sought out!
7 All your allies have driven you to your border;
   those at peace with you have deceived you;
they have prevailed against you;
   those who eat your bread[c] have set a trap beneath you—
   you have[d] no understanding.
8 Will I not on that day, declares the Lord,
   destroy the wise men out of Edom,
   and understanding out of Mount Esau?
9 And your mighty men shall be dismayed, O Teman,
   so that every man from Mount Esau will be cut off by slaughter.

Edom's Violence Against Jacob

10 Because of the violence done to your brother Jacob,
   shame shall cover you,
   and you shall be cut off forever.
11 On the day that you stood aloof,
   on the day that strangers carried off his wealth
and foreigners entered his gates
   and cast lots for Jerusalem,
   you were like one of them.
12 But do not gloat over the day of your brother
   in the day of his misfortune;
do not rejoice over the people of Judah
   in the day of their ruin;
do not boast[e]
   in the day of distress.
13 Do not enter the gate of my people
   in the day of their calamity;
do not gloat over his disaster
   in the day of his calamity;
do not loot his wealth
   in the day of his calamity.
14 Do not stand at the crossroads
   to cut off his fugitives;

LESSON 1:
CAUSE OF THE BATTLE OF THE FLESH & CONSEQUENCES; COVENANT FOR ABRAHAM FOR BELIEVERS—STRUGGLE OF THE FLESH

> do not hand over his survivors
>   in the day of distress.
> The Day of the Lord Is Near
> [15] For the day of the Lord is near upon all the nations.
> As you have done, it shall be done to you;
>   your deeds shall return on your own head.
> [16] For as you have drunk on my holy mountain,
>   so all the nations shall drink continually;
> they shall drink and swallow,
>   and shall be as though they had never been.

_____
_____
_____
_____
_____

What is the message of this? There's a difference between living in the Spirit, and thus receiving the Covenant, to thrive and be blessed (Jacob) and living in the flesh, not receiving the Covenant, not thriving and not being blessed. (Esau and his life being worthless). And we have a choice, as did Esau, who sold his birthright and thus despised the Covenant. They both could have been blessed, but even though they were members of God's family, their experience of the abundant life was quite different—based upon the choice of—living in the flesh or living in the Spirit. (See this further explained in Hebrews.)

Read through these verses and write out why God did not accept Esau's supposed repentance. How might we understand this for our lives today?

> **Read Hebrews 12:12–17:**
>
> [12] Therefore lift your drooping hands and strengthen your weak knees, [13] and make straight paths for your feet, so that what is lame may not be put out of joint but rather be healed. [14] Strive for peace with everyone, and for the holiness without which no one will see the Lord. [15] See to it that no one fails to obtain the grace of God; that no "root of bitterness" springs up and causes trouble, and by it many become defiled; [16] that no one is sexually immoral

LESSON 1:
CAUSE OF THE BATTLE OF THE FLESH & CONSEQUENCES; COVENANT FOR ABRAHAM FOR BELIEVERS—STRUGGLE OF THE FLESH

> or unholy like Esau, who sold his birthright for a single meal. [17] For you know that afterward, when he desired to inherit the blessing, he was rejected, for he found no chance to repent, though he sought it with tears.

_____
_____
_____
_____
_____

He states that we are not to be unholy, like Esau who gave up his Covenant right by choosing to live in the flesh. The writers of the New Testament believed these to be symbols: Esau is flesh, and Jacob is spirit. (We will continue to see that Jacob had his own issues with the flesh, which implies that it is a continual process of choosing to deny self, take up the cross, and follow Him in the Spirit.)

In this situation, it says that Esau, who sought repentance, was not allowed. Based upon our understanding of the character of God, this does not seem right. How could this be? Since the nature of God is always to receive us upon true repentance, what must be going on here? Esau did not really repent. He only sought the blessing, not the blesser. He said, "I would like what I gave up," while still despising the Covenant since he was not willing to follow God. "Just give me what I desire still. I'm going to do my own thing continually, even out of the desire to receive the blessings. I'll try to do things to please God." But, of course, it is deeper than that: a heart that chooses to live in the Spirit versus living in the flesh.

LESSON 2:
DIFFERENCE BETWEEN ESAU (REPRESENTING LIFE IN THE FLESH) AND JACOB (REPRESENTING LIFE IN THE SPIRIT)

> "As believers, we must be in Christ and choose to live in the Spirit and receive the Covenant."

For this lesson we're going to continue with this discussion of the battle of the flesh versus the Spirit. We've set up the premise in Lesson 1 that we do have an issue, and Paul describes this in Romans. He says: "I find a law that's operating. I have a heart to follow God, but I tend to act in the flesh (self, deciding my own will); I can't fulfill living righteously on my own. It's not possible." And so, we understand that we have this battle. Unfortunately, we have it every single day because our sin nature isn't getting better. It has to be put to death every day. With this issue, is there any hope for this? And is there any opportunity for us to live the life of the Spirit? Yes! As we learned in Lesson 1 through the life of Abraham, Isaac, and Jacob, that through Abraham, this Covenant (promise) has been passed on to Jesus, who's now the sole recipient (remember, it said seed not seeds). As believers, we must be in Christ and choose to live in the Spirit and receive the Covenant (the promises He has planned for us personally).

We further discussed Esau and Jacob; and how Esau despised the promise because he despised the Covenant, and ultimately rejected it by choosing his own way. This, then, represents living in the flesh. Jacob represents living in the Spirit, though he, too, was not perfect (as none of us is) and struggled with the flesh versus the Spirit (our universal battle).

Read through these verses and write out why God continually had Isaac move from place to place. What do you understand about the wiles, strategies, and tactics of the enemy? How does this affect us?

> **Read Genesis 26:1–35:**
>
> God's Promise to Isaac
> **26** Now there was a famine in the land, besides the former famine that was in the days of Abraham. And Isaac went to Gerar to Abimelech king of the Philistines. ² And the Lord appeared to him and said, "Do not go down to Egypt; dwell in the land of which I shall tell you. ³ Sojourn

LESSON 2:
DIFFERENCE BETWEEN ESAU (REPRESENTING LIFE IN THE FLESH) AND JACOB (REPRESENTING LIFE IN THE SPIRIT)

in this land, and I will be with you and will bless you, for to you and to your offspring I will give all these lands, and I will establish the oath that I swore to Abraham your father. 4 I will multiply your offspring as the stars of heaven and will give to your offspring all these lands. And in your offspring all the nations of the earth shall be blessed, 5 because Abraham obeyed my voice and kept my charge, my commandments, my statutes, and my laws."

Isaac and Abimelech

6 So Isaac settled in Gerar. 7 When the men of the place asked him about his wife, he said, "She is my sister," for he feared to say, "My wife," thinking, "lest the men of the place should kill me because of Rebekah," because she was attractive in appearance. 8 When he had been there a long time, Abimelech, king of the Philistines looked out of a window and saw Isaac laughing with[a] Rebekah his wife. 9 So Abimelech called Isaac and said, "Behold, she is your wife. How then could you say, 'She is my sister'?" Isaac said to him, "Because I thought, 'Lest I die because of her.'" 10 Abimelech said, "What is this you have done to us? One of the people might easily have lain with your wife, and you would have brought guilt upon us." 11 So Abimelech warned all the people, saying, "Whoever touches this man or his wife shall surely be put to death."

12 And Isaac sowed in that land and reaped in the same year a hundredfold. The Lord blessed him, 13 and the man became rich, and gained more and more until he became very wealthy. 14 He had possessions of flocks and herds and many servants, so that the Philistines envied him. 15 (Now the Philistines had stopped and filled with earth all the wells that his father's servants had dug in the days of Abraham his father.) 16 And Abimelech said to Isaac, "Go away from us, for you are much mightier than we."

17 So Isaac departed from there and encamped in the Valley of Gerar and settled there. 18 And Isaac dug again the wells of water that had been dug in the days of Abraham his father, which the Philistines had stopped after the death of Abraham. And he gave them the names that his father had given them. 19 But when Isaac's servants dug in the valley and found there a well of spring water, 20 the herdsmen of Gerar quarreled with Isaac's herdsmen, saying, "The water is ours." So he called the name of the well Esek,[b] because they contended with him. 21 Then they dug another well, and they quarreled over that also, so he called its name Sitnah.[c] 22 And he moved from there and dug another well, and they did not quarrel over it. So he called its name Rehoboth,[d] saying, "For now the Lord has made room for us, and we shall be fruitful in the land."

LESSON 2:
DIFFERENCE BETWEEN ESAU (REPRESENTING LIFE IN THE FLESH) AND JACOB (REPRESENTING LIFE IN THE SPIRIT)

> 23 From there he went up to Beersheba. 24 And the Lord appeared to him the same night and said, "I am the God of Abraham your father. Fear not, for I am with you and will bless you and multiply your offspring for my servant Abraham's sake." 25 So he built an altar there and called upon the name of the Lord and pitched his tent there. And there Isaac's servants dug a well.
>
> 26 When Abimelech went to him from Gerar with Ahuzzath his adviser and Phicol the commander of his army, 27 Isaac said to them, "Why have you come to me, seeing that you hate me and have sent me away from you?" 28 They said, "We see plainly that the Lord has been with you. So we said, let there be a sworn pact between us, between you and us, and let us make a Covenant with you, 29 that you will do us no harm, just as we have not touched you and have done to you nothing but good and have sent you away in peace. You are now the blessed of the Lord." 30 So he made them a feast, and they ate and drank. 31 In the morning they rose early and exchanged oaths. And Isaac sent them on their way, and they departed from him in peace. 32 That same day Isaac's servants came and told him about the well that they had dug and said to him, "We have found water." 33 He called it Shibah;[e] therefore the name of the city is Beersheba to this day.
>
> 34 When Esau was forty years old, he took Judith the daughter of Beeri the Hittite to be his wife, and Basemath the daughter of Elon the Hittite, 35 and they made life bitter[f] for Isaac and Rebekah.

_____
_____
_____
_____
_____

That's a soap opera, isn't it? Let's first look at Isaac. What is God doing? He's blessing him. And it says one hundred–fold, which means it's magnificent, it's over–the–top, spectacular, and he's receiving wonderful provision. The enemy then works to destroy this blessing, through a tricky strategy, by taking over his wells, the necessary source of water. "If I can take your water, you either fight me or you have to leave. God is blessing him, so the enemy wants to do what? Kill, steal, and destroy. Isaac could either fight or leave. He understood from God that he had to leave and that God would bless him in another place with wells/water. He had a right to fight and even ask God to prevail, but God said to leave, and since Isaac surrendered to God's will, he followed the One who knew best.

LESSON 2:
DIFFERENCE BETWEEN ESAU (REPRESENTING LIFE IN THE FLESH) AND JACOB (REPRESENTING LIFE IN THE SPIRIT)

This is a representation of not looking at things logically, but rather in the Spirit. Instead of using logic to make decisions, we are to follow God who knows all, and wants us to experience His best. Why? We are children of the Covenant, and He will deliver the Covenant to us. We will be blessed to be a blessing.

But the enemy is relentless, and as Isaac moved from place to place, so the enemy came to fight for occupation of that place to continue his nature of kill, steal, and destroy. But Isaac continued to follow God, who promised to deliver His Covenant, and went to the next place, and the next place, and continued to be blessed.

Then something interesting happened. The enemy noticed that wherever Isaac went (after being chased away from each location), he was being blessed by God. So, they decided that perhaps they could coexist, and if they stayed together in the same location, maybe they might be blessed along with Isaac. Interestingly, this is the essence of the Covenant: blessed to be a blessing, and God will bless those who bless you and curse those who curse you. It's all about their response to you—either cooperating, supporting, or opposing.

At the end of this story, what did Esau do? He disobeyed. As part of the Covenant, he was to marry within the community; and not to marry into the enemy camp. But Esau rejected this truth, and he married into the enemy. Why? The same reason that Esau sold his birthright. He didn't care about it. He despised it, rejecting the Covenant again (and revealing why his supposed repentance that we discussed in Lesson 1 was not real). We will see more consequences of this later.

Read through these verses and write out how Jacob and Rebecca deceived Isaac. With this deception, how could Jacob actually be the recipient of the blessing? What does this mean for us?

> **Read Genesis 27:1–40:**
>
> Isaac Blesses Jacob
> **27** When Isaac was old and his eyes were dim so that he could not see, he called Esau his older son and said to him, "My son"; and he answered, "Here I am." [2] He said, "Behold, I am old; I do not know the day of my death. [3] Now then, take your weapons, your quiver and your bow, and go out to the field and hunt game for me, [4] and prepare for me delicious food, such as I love, and bring it to me so that I may eat, that my soul may bless you before I die."
>
> [5] Now Rebekah was listening when Isaac spoke to his son Esau. So when Esau went to the field to hunt for game and bring it, [6] Rebekah said to her son Jacob, "I heard your father speak to your brother Esau, [7] 'Bring me game and prepare

LESSON 2:
DIFFERENCE BETWEEN ESAU (REPRESENTING LIFE IN THE FLESH) AND JACOB (REPRESENTING LIFE IN THE SPIRIT)

for me delicious food, that I may eat it and bless you before the Lord before I die.' [8] Now therefore, my son, obey my voice as I command you. [9] Go to the flock and bring me two good young goats, so that I may prepare from them delicious food for your father, such as he loves. [10] And you shall bring it to your father to eat, so that he may bless you before he dies." [11] But Jacob said to Rebekah his mother, "Behold, my brother Esau is a hairy man, and I am a smooth man. [12] Perhaps my father will feel me, and I shall seem to be mocking him and bring a curse upon myself and not a blessing." [13] His mother said to him, "Let your curse be on me, my son; only obey my voice, and go, bring them to me."

[14] So he went and took them and brought them to his mother, and his mother prepared delicious food, such as his father loved. [15] Then Rebekah took the best garments of Esau her older son, which were with her in the house, and put them on Jacob her younger son. [16] And the skins of the young goats she put on his hands and on the smooth part of his neck. [17] And she put the delicious food and the bread, which she had prepared, into the hand of her son Jacob.

[18] So he went in to his father and said, "My father." And he said, "Here I am. Who are you, my son?" [19] Jacob said to his father, "I am Esau your firstborn. I have done as you told me; now sit up and eat of my game, that your soul may bless me." [20] But Isaac said to his son, "How is it that you have found it so quickly, my son?" He answered, "Because the Lord your God granted me success." [21] Then Isaac said to Jacob, "Please come near, that I may feel you, my son, to know whether you are really my son Esau or not." [22] So Jacob went near to Isaac his father, who felt him and said, "The voice is Jacob's voice, but the hands are the hands of Esau." [23] And he did not recognize him, because his hands were hairy like his brother Esau's hands. So he blessed him. [24] He said, "Are you really my son Esau?" He answered, "I am." [25] Then he said, "Bring it near to me, that I may eat of my son's game and bless you." So he brought it near to him, and he ate; and he brought him wine, and he drank.

[26] Then his father Isaac said to him, "Come near and kiss me, my son." [27] So he came near and kissed him. And Isaac smelled the smell of his garments and blessed him and said,

"See, the smell of my son
   is as the smell of a field that the Lord has blessed!
[28] May God give you of the dew of heaven
   and of the fatness of the earth
   and plenty of grain and wine.
[29] Let peoples serve you,
   and nations bow down to you.

LESSON 2:
DIFFERENCE BETWEEN ESAU (REPRESENTING LIFE IN THE FLESH) AND JACOB (REPRESENTING LIFE IN THE SPIRIT)

Be lord over your brothers,
   and may your mother's sons bow down to you.
Cursed be everyone who curses you,
   and blessed be everyone who blesses you!"

30 As soon as Isaac had finished blessing Jacob, when Jacob had scarcely gone out from the presence of Isaac his father, Esau his brother came in from his hunting. 31 He also prepared delicious food and brought it to his father. And he said to his father, "Let my father arise and eat of his son's game, that you may bless me." 32 His father Isaac said to him, "Who are you?" He answered, "I am your son, your firstborn, Esau." 33 Then Isaac trembled very violently and said, "Who was it then that hunted game and brought it to me, and I ate it all before you came, and I have blessed him? Yes, and he shall be blessed." 34 As soon as Esau heard the words of his father, he cried out with an exceedingly great and bitter cry and said to his father, "Bless me, even me also, O my father!" 35 But he said, "Your brother came deceitfully, and he has taken away your blessing." 36 Esau said, "Is he not rightly named Jacob?[a] For he has cheated me these two times. He took away my birthright, and behold, now he has taken away my blessing." Then he said, "Have you not reserved a blessing for me?" 37 Isaac answered and said to Esau, "Behold, I have made him lord over you, and all his brothers I have given to him for servants, and with grain and wine I have sustained him. What then can I do for you, my son?" 38 Esau said to his father, "Have you but one blessing, my father? Bless me, even me also, O my father." And Esau lifted up his voice and wept.

39 Then Isaac his father answered and said to him:
"Behold, away from[b] the fatness of the earth shall your dwelling be,
   and away from[c] the dew of heaven on high.
40 By your sword you shall live,
   and you shall serve your brother;
but when you grow restless
   you shall break his yoke from your neck."

_____
_____
_____
_____
_____

LESSON 2:
DIFFERENCE BETWEEN ESAU (REPRESENTING LIFE IN THE FLESH) AND JACOB (REPRESENTING LIFE IN THE SPIRIT)

The soap opera continues. Jacob and Rebecca deceived Isaac. At the moment, Jacob is living as a deceiver. He goes through with this elaborate ruse, but he gets blessed. So, the question is that, in the deception, why did Isaac honor the blessing? He spoke it. He gave it, and he honored what he gave, even though the recipient wasn't really the rightful recipient. It was through deception that he received it, but because of honor, as it was given. So, would you call Jacob spiritual? No, he's not. But there is something that God knows about him. What does he know about Jacob? He has a heart for God. Remember what God said about David when He selected David as the next king after Saul rejected God and the Covenant. (Look at Acts 13:16–25 where God speaks of David as a man after God's own heart).

Was David perfect? No. So, we're starting to see that the Covenant and walking in the Spirit is not about perfection. Even when there's deception, God knows the heart.

The blessings are not dependent upon being perfect (thank goodness), but upon our heart—a heart to follow God and live in the Spirit.

Read through these two sets of verses and write out the difference between receiving God's blessing and not receiving God's blessings. Why is this important for us?

> **Read Deuteronomy 28:1–14:**
>
> Blessings for Obedience
> **28** "And if you faithfully obey the voice of the Lord your God, being careful to do all his commandments that I command you today, the Lord your God will set you high above all the nations of the earth. 2 And all these blessings shall come upon you and overtake you, if you obey the voice of the Lord your God. 3 Blessed shall you be in the city, and blessed shall you be in the field. 4 Blessed shall be the fruit of your womb and the fruit of your ground and the fruit of your cattle, the increase of your herds and the young of your flock. 5 Blessed shall be your basket and your kneading bowl. 6 Blessed shall you be when you come in, and blessed shall you be when you go out.
>
> 7 "The Lord will cause your enemies who rise against you to be defeated before you. They shall come out against you one way and flee before you seven ways. 8 The Lord will command the blessing on you in your barns and in all that you undertake. And he will bless you in the land that the Lord your God is giving you. 9 The Lord will establish you as a people holy to himself, as he has sworn to you, if you keep the commandments of the Lord your God and walk in his ways. 10 And all the peoples of the earth shall see that you are called by the name of the Lord, and they shall be afraid of you. 11 And the Lord will make you abound in prosperity, in the fruit of your womb and in the fruit of your

LESSON 2:
DIFFERENCE BETWEEN ESAU (REPRESENTING LIFE IN THE FLESH) AND JACOB (REPRESENTING LIFE IN THE SPIRIT)

> livestock and in the fruit of your ground, within the land that the Lord swore to your fathers to give you. ¹² The Lord will open to you his good treasury, the heavens, to give the rain to your land in its season and to bless all the work of your hands. And you shall lend to many nations, but you shall not borrow. ¹³ And the Lord will make you the head and not the tail, and you shall only go up and not down, if you obey the commandments of the Lord your God, which I command you today, being careful to do them, ¹⁴ and if you do not turn aside from any of the words that I command you today, to the right hand or to the left, to go after other gods to serve them.

_____
_____
_____
_____
_____

This states that if we hear and follow God, we will receive blessings: the promises of the fourteen verses of blessings. These blessings are promised if we: "Walk with Me, stay with Me—walking in the Spirit"; and then the blessings will overtake us. Our focus isn't on the blessings. Which, by the way, is the problem with Esau. When he said, "Hey, I'd like the blessing anyway," he didn't care about God. He just wanted the blessing. God says, "As soon as you turn around and look at the blessing, it stops. The key is to keep walking with Me, seek Me, follow Me—not the blessing—and when this is true of your heart, the blessings overtake you."

> **Read Deuteronomy 28:15:**
>
> Curses for Disobedience
> ¹⁵ "But if you will not obey the voice of the Lord your God or be careful to do all his commandments and his statutes that I command you today, then all these curses shall come upon you and overtake you.

_____
_____
_____
_____
_____

LESSON 2:
DIFFERENCE BETWEEN ESAU (REPRESENTING LIFE IN THE FLESH) AND JACOB (REPRESENTING LIFE IN THE SPIRIT)

If we choose not to follow God, we will not receive the promised blessings of the Covenant; and will actually experience more difficult circumstances of life. This would be our own choice. As in Deuteronomy 30:10–20, God sets before us life or death, blessings or curses. Are you willing to follow Him or not? It's your choice. It's guaranteed that He's going to bless you to make you a blessing if you have a heart to follow. And that's what He gave to Jacob. And God knew that Jacob's heart, even though at this moment was deceitful, was a heart that desired to follow God, which was the key (not being perfect but a heart to learn to and then follow God).

So, because Jacob was the recipient of the blessing, Esau got upset and requested that he get the blessing anyway. Though he was no longer the recipient of the Covenant, or his birthright, which he has despised and sold, Isaac did offer the blessing anyway. Because Esau has despised God and the Covenant, and married into the enemy in rebellion, he responds in anger to what he considers to be a lesser blessing. To the extent that he says, "What? I'm going to kill Jacob as soon as Dad dies." What kind of response is that? Flesh. Where's the heart at? Is that a heart to follow God? No. If he had sought God and understood anything about the Covenant, he could have been blessed by just staying in concert with and in partnership with Jacob. He would have been blessed. He could have truly repented and asked God to help him understand how he could enjoy this blessing as well. Instead, because of flesh, which was expressed in anger, he was intent on killing Jacob. That's where a lot of believers are in the flesh. Mad, mad, mad. God didn't do this. God didn't do that. God didn't... How come? How come others are lucky, and I'm not? We then remain in the flesh and disqualify us to be the recipient of the Covenant. This is about our heart.

Because of Esau's desire to kill Jacob, God, through Rebecca, sends him to Laban, who lives in a completely different place. Go, be with him, and wait—and as part of receiving God's planned blessing, it is important to marry into his own community—have a heart to follow God. Maybe Esau will soften up?

Read through these verses and write out the difference between Esau and Jacob. How does this apply to our lives?

> **Read Genesis 28:1–9:**
>
> **Jacob Sent to Laban**
> **28** Then Isaac called Jacob and blessed him and directed him, "You must not take a wife from the Canaanite women. ² Arise, go to Paddan-aram to the house of Bethuel your mother's father, and take as your wife from there one of the daughters of Laban your mother's brother. ³ God Almighty[a] bless you

LESSON 2:
DIFFERENCE BETWEEN ESAU (REPRESENTING LIFE IN THE FLESH) AND JACOB (REPRESENTING LIFE IN THE SPIRIT)

> and make you fruitful and multiply you, that you may become a company of peoples. ⁴ May he give the blessing of Abraham to you and to your offspring with you, that you may take possession of the land of your sojournings that God gave to Abraham!" ⁵ Thus Isaac sent Jacob away. And he went to Paddan-aram, to Laban, the son of Bethuel the Aramean, the brother of Rebekah, Jacob's and Esau's mother.
>
> Esau Marries an Ishmaelite
> ⁶ Now Esau saw that Isaac had blessed Jacob and sent him away to Paddan-aram to take a wife from there, and that as he blessed him he directed him, "You must not take a wife from the Canaanite women," ⁷ and that Jacob had obeyed his father and his mother and gone to Paddan-aram. ⁸ So when Esau saw that the Canaanite women did not please Isaac his father, ⁹ Esau went to Ishmael and took as his wife, besides the wives he had, Mahalath the daughter of Ishmael, Abraham's son, the sister of Nebaioth.

_____
_____
_____
_____
_____

    With his admonition to go to Laban and marry within his family, Jacob agrees to follow the direction by moving there and looking for a wife. His heart was to experience the Covenant and follow the direction of the Lord. Esau goes the opposite direction; having already married into the enemy, he decides to move farther away, and pursue a wife farther away from Abraham's, Isaac's and Jacob's God—in Ishmael. We see again this structure of our study: Esau represents living in the flesh, and Jacob represents living in the Spirit. Self-centeredness versus God-centeredness. And, why does Esau walk farther away from God? He has a hardening of the heart, where he despises the Covenant and blames God for not giving him the Covenant as a guarantee. As a child of God, underneath it all, you are angry at Him. Your heart gets harder and harder toward God, you blame Him, and you're angry at Him. And so, you just keep going farther and farther away in your hardness. Why? Because you're not wanting to follow Him, you're despising Him. Why? That's where the flesh goes, absent of walking in the Spirit.

LESSON 2:
DIFFERENCE BETWEEN ESAU (REPRESENTING LIFE IN THE FLESH) AND JACOB (REPRESENTING LIFE IN THE SPIRIT)

Read through these sets of verses and write out the meaning of Jacob's dream. Why is this so important to highlight in scripture, both in the Old Testament and the New Testament? And why is this significant to us?

> **Read Genesis 28:10–22:**
>
> Jacob's Dream
> [10] Jacob left Beersheba and went toward Haran. [11] And he came to a certain place and stayed there that night, because the sun had set. Taking one of the stones of the place, he put it under his head and lay down in that place to sleep. [12] And he dreamed, and behold, there was a ladder[a] set up on the earth, and the top of it reached to heaven. And behold, the angels of God were ascending and descending on it! [13] And behold, the Lord stood above it[b] and said, "I am the Lord, the God of Abraham your father and the God of Isaac. The land on which you lie I will give to you and to your offspring. [14] Your offspring shall be like the dust of the earth, and you shall spread abroad to the west and to the east and to the north and to the south, and in you and your offspring shall all the families of the earth be blessed. [15] Behold, I am with you and will keep you wherever you go, and will bring you back to this land. For I will not leave you until I have done what I have promised you." [16] Then Jacob awoke from his sleep and said, "Surely the Lord is in this place, and I did not know it." [17] And he was afraid and said, "How awesome is this place! This is none other than the house of God, and this is the gate of heaven."
>
> [18] So early in the morning Jacob took the stone that he had put under his head and set it up for a pillar and poured oil on the top of it. [19] He called the name of that place Bethel,[c] but the name of the city was Luz at the first. [20] Then Jacob made a vow, saying, "If God will be with me and will keep me in this way that I go, and will give me bread to eat and clothing to wear, [21] so that I come again to my father's house in peace, then the Lord shall be my God, [22] and this stone, which I have set up for a pillar, shall be God's house. And of all that you give me I will give a full tenth to you."

_____
_____
_____
_____
_____

LESSON 2:
DIFFERENCE BETWEEN ESAU (REPRESENTING LIFE IN THE FLESH) AND JACOB (REPRESENTING LIFE IN THE SPIRIT)

This is the wonderful story of Jacob's Ladder. Jacob had a dream. He saw this ladder go from Earth to what? The bottom of the ladder set on the Earth, and the top of the ladder reached heaven. What is God showing Jacob? His life isn't just here, it's connected to the spiritual, and God is in both places. The two are connected. In other words, it's not when you die or at some distant part of your life, it's here, now. It's connected. The life of the spiritual is connected here to the natural. And God gives Jacob an incredible revelation and a dream.

Side note: How significant are dreams? Very. God is able to reveal something because your conscious isn't in the way to reject it, and it can go right to your subconscious or your soul. When the Spirit wakes you up and has you remember consciously the dream, He has something to reveal to you, a message. Keep a notepad by your bed so that when you wake up, you can write down all the details. Even if you are certain you will remember it clearly—you won't. You need to write it down when you wake up—when all the details are vivid to you. Then the next morning, ask God to give you the interpretation.

Understand that it is always simple, a message to you, not something by which you are to live your life according to the details that you try to figure out. You do not need a book that someone has put together to tell you the meaning of certain colors, or the meaning of certain numbers, or the meaning of certain situations. God is much more creative than a system, and He is not limited to any natural way of expressing His revelations to you. Mostly, understand that there's connectivity between the spiritual and the natural and that this is the essence of the Covenant. Blessed to be a blessing happens in God's Kingdom, in the spiritual place as it is then expressed in the natural where you live on Jacob's Ladder! But there is more of this to learn:

Read John 1:29–51:

Behold, the Lamb of God
[29] The next day he saw Jesus coming toward him, and said, "Behold, the Lamb of God, who takes away the sin of the world! [30] This is he of whom I said, 'After me comes a man who ranks before me, because he was before me.' [31] I myself did not know him, but for this purpose I came baptizing with water, that he might be revealed to Israel." [32] And John bore witness: "I saw the Spirit descend from heaven like a dove, and it remained on him. [33] I myself did not know him, but he who sent me to baptize with water said to me, 'He on whom you see the Spirit descend and remain, this is he who baptizes with the Holy Spirit.' [34] And I have seen and have borne witness that this is the Son[a] of God."

LESSON 2:
DIFFERENCE BETWEEN ESAU (REPRESENTING LIFE IN THE FLESH) AND JACOB (REPRESENTING LIFE IN THE SPIRIT)

Jesus Calls the First Disciples

35 The next day again John was standing with two of his disciples, 36 and he looked at Jesus as he walked by and said, "Behold, the Lamb of God!" 37 The two disciples heard him say this, and they followed Jesus. 38 Jesus turned and saw them following and said to them, "What are you seeking?" And they said to him, "Rabbi" (which means Teacher), "where are you staying?" 39 He said to them, "Come and you will see." So they came and saw where he was staying, and they stayed with him that day, for it was about the tenth hour.[b] 40 One of the two who heard John speak and followed Jesus[c] was Andrew, Simon Peter's brother. 41 He first found his own brother Simon and said to him, "We have found the Messiah" (which means Christ). 42 He brought him to Jesus. Jesus looked at him and said, "You are Simon the son of John. You shall be called Cephas" (which means Peter[d]).

Jesus Calls Philip and Nathanael

43 The next day Jesus decided to go to Galilee. He found Philip and said to him, "Follow me." 44 Now Philip was from Bethsaida, the city of Andrew and Peter. 45 Philip found Nathanael and said to him, "We have found him of whom Moses in the Law and also the prophets wrote, Jesus of Nazareth, the son of Joseph." 46 Nathanael said to him, "Can anything good come out of Nazareth?" Philip said to him, "Come and see." 47 Jesus saw Nathanael coming toward him and said of him, "Behold, an Israelite indeed, in whom there is no deceit!" 48 Nathanael said to him, "How do you know me?" Jesus answered him, "Before Philip called you, when you were under the fig tree, I saw you." 49 Nathanael answered him, "Rabbi, you are the Son of God! You are the King of Israel!" 50 Jesus answered him, "Because I said to you, 'I saw you under the fig tree,' do you believe? You will see greater things than these." 51 And he said to him, "Truly, truly, I say to you,[e] you will see heaven opened, and the angels of God ascending and descending on the Son of Man."

_____
_____
_____
_____
_____

LESSON 2:
DIFFERENCE BETWEEN ESAU (REPRESENTING LIFE IN THE FLESH) AND JACOB (REPRESENTING LIFE IN THE SPIRIT)

This is describing the calling of the disciples and Jesus' invitation to come and follow Him, to experience Him and the life He brings. And then He says: What you're going to experience is the angels ascending and descending, coming to Earth from the spiritual. And the spiritual is going to connect to the natural. This is Jacob's Ladder. Who is Jacob's Ladder? Christ, who is connecting the spiritual heaven with the natural. Jacob was given the privilege of seeing this wonderful truth, that we here on Earth, in the physical, are connected through God Himself with the spiritual Kingdom, and thus have all the power of the spiritual Kingdom. Let's understand this further:

> **Read Hebrews 1:5–2:4:**
>
> 5 For to which of the angels did God ever say,
> "You are my Son,
>   today I have begotten you"?
>
> Or again,
> "I will be to him a father,
>   and he shall be to me a son"?
>
> 6 And again, when he brings the firstborn into the world, he says,
> "Let all God's angels worship him."
>
> 7 Of the angels he says,
> "He makes his angels winds,
>   and his ministers a flame of fire."
>
> 8 But of the Son he says,
> "Your throne, O God, is forever and ever,
>   the scepter of uprightness is the scepter of your kingdom.
> 9 You have loved righteousness and hated wickedness;
> therefore God, your God, has anointed you
>   with the oil of gladness beyond your companions."
>
> 10 And,
> "You, Lord, laid the foundation of the earth in the beginning,
>   and the heavens are the work of your hands;
> 11 they will perish, but you remain;
>   they will all wear out like a garment,
> 12 like a robe you will roll them up,
>   like a garment they will be changed.[a]
> But you are the same,
>   and your years will have no end."

LESSON 2:
DIFFERENCE BETWEEN ESAU (REPRESENTING LIFE IN THE FLESH) AND JACOB (REPRESENTING LIFE IN THE SPIRIT)

> [13] And to which of the angels has he ever said,
> "Sit at my right hand
>   until I make your enemies a footstool for your feet"?
>
> [14] Are they not all ministering spirits sent out to serve for the sake of those who are to inherit salvation?
>
> Warning Against Neglecting Salvation
> **2** Therefore we must pay much closer attention to what we have heard, lest we drift away from it. [2] For since the message declared by angels proved to be reliable, and every transgression or disobedience received a just retribution, [3] how shall we escape if we neglect such a great salvation? It was declared at first by the Lord, and it was attested to us by those who heard, [4] while God also bore witness by signs and wonders and various miracles and by gifts of the Holy Spirit distributed according to his will.

LESSON 3:
JACOB'S BATTLE OF THE FLESH, EXPERIENCE OF VICTORY OVER THE FLESH, GOD'S FAITHFULNESS DESPITE THE FLESH

> "...he invites us to live in the Spirit where the beautiful life is that God wants to deliver to us."

As we begin Lesson 3, let's summarize where we've been in the battle of the flesh versus the Spirit as we've studied the life of Jacob. Our premise is based upon what Paul has spoken to us in Romans 7: There's a law, an issue with the flesh, and no matter how hard we try, all the work that we try to do on our own, we're not able to fulfill it. And he said there's a distinguishing factor between living in the flesh and living in the Spirit as a believer. If we live in the flesh (self and self-determination), we are at enmity against God, we put to death the work of the Spirit and we cannot please God. So, he invites us to live in the Spirit where the beautiful life is that God wants to deliver to us. As we've gotten into the life of Jacob, we've seen a couple of key things:

- The Amalekite's and the descendants from Esau represent the flesh. Esau despised the Covenant. He despised his blessing because he didn't care about it (neglected so great a salvation).

- He's at enmity against God and not willing to follow God.

- Whereas Jacob, who also has some issues as a young believer and isn't mature yet, is learning what it means to follow God.

- God looks at the heart. It's not about being perfect, it's about the heart. Do you have a heart to follow God?

- We've learned some lessons with Jacob's Ladder. There's a connectivity between heaven (spiritual Kingdom) and Earth, and we live in both places. Christ reiterates it as He calls His disciples to come and follow Him. He says, I am the ladder. So, the connecting point is Jesus.

LESSON 3:
JACOB'S BATTLE OF THE FLESH, EXPERIENCE OF VICTORY OVER THE FLESH, GOD'S FAITHFULNESS DESPITE THE FLESH

Read through these sets of verses and write out the role of the flesh in the life of Jacob. What caused this, and what were the consequences of this? Why did Jacob continue to honor his commitments even though deceit was involved? Why is that significant to us? What are the benefits of operating with integrity, and how are we to carry this out?

Read Genesis 29:1–30:

Jacob Marries Leah and Rachel
29 Then Jacob went on his journey and came to the land of the people of the east. ² As he looked, he saw a well in the field, and behold, three flocks of sheep lying beside it, for out of that well the flocks were watered. The stone on the well's mouth was large, ³ and when all the flocks were gathered there, the shepherds would roll the stone from the mouth of the well and water the sheep, and put the stone back in its place over the mouth of the well.

⁴ Jacob said to them, "My brothers, where do you come from?" They said "We are from Haran." ⁵ He said to them, "Do you know Laban the son of Nahor?" They said, "We know him." ⁶ He said to them, "Is it well with him?" They said, "It is well; and see, Rachel his daughter is coming with the sheep!" ⁷ He said, "Behold, it is still high day; it is not time for the livestock to be gathered together. Water the sheep and go, pasture them." ⁸ But they said, "We cannot until all the flocks are gathered together and the stone is rolled from the mouth of the well; then we water the sheep."

⁹ While he was still speaking with them, Rachel came with her father's sheep, for she was a shepherdess. ¹⁰ Now as soon as Jacob saw Rachel the daughter of Laban his mother's brother, and the sheep of Laban his mother's brother, Jacob came near and rolled the stone from the well's mouth and watered the flock of Laban his mother's brother. ¹¹ Then Jacob kissed Rachel and wept aloud. ¹² And Jacob told Rachel that he was her father's kinsman, and that he was Rebekah's son, and she ran and told her father.

¹³ As soon as Laban heard the news about Jacob, his sister's son, he ran to meet him and embraced him and kissed him and brought him to his house. Jacob told Laban all these things, ¹⁴ and Laban said to him, "Surely you are my bone and my flesh!" And he stayed with him a month.

¹⁵ Then Laban said to Jacob, "Because you are my kinsman, should you therefore serve me for nothing? Tell me, what shall your wages be?" ¹⁶ Now Laban had two daughters. The name of the older was Leah, and the name of the younger was Rachel. ¹⁷ Leah's eyes were weak,[a] but Rachel was beautiful in form and

LESSON 3:
JACOB'S BATTLE OF THE FLESH, EXPERIENCE OF VICTORY OVER THE FLESH, GOD'S FAITHFULNESS DESPITE THE FLESH

> appearance. [18] Jacob loved Rachel. And he said, "I will serve you seven years for your younger daughter Rachel." [19] Laban said, "It is better that I give her to you than that I should give her to any other man; stay with me." [20] So Jacob served seven years for Rachel, and they seemed to him but a few days because of the love he had for her.
>
> [21] Then Jacob said to Laban, "Give me my wife that I may go in to her, for my time is completed." [22] So Laban gathered together all the people of the place and made a feast. [23] But in the evening he took his daughter Leah and brought her to Jacob, and he went in to her. [24] (Laban gave[b] his female servant Zilpah to his daughter Leah to be her servant.) [25] And in the morning, behold, it was Leah! And Jacob said to Laban, "What is this you have done to me? Did I not serve with you for Rachel? Why then have you deceived me?" [26] Laban said, "It is not so done in our country, to give the younger before the firstborn. [27] Complete the week of this one, and we will give you the other also in return for serving me another seven years." [28] Jacob did so, and completed her week. Then Laban gave him his daughter Rachel to be his wife. [29] (Laban gave his female servant Bilhah to his daughter Rachel to be her servant.) [30] So Jacob went in to Rachel also, and he loved Rachel more than Leah, and served Laban for another seven years.

_____
_____
_____
_____
_____

    This family is also a soap opera. They're all tricksters—excellent examples of the flesh—manipulators, and full of deceit. So, what was the cost to Jacob to get to the point of marrying Rachel? Fourteen years of serving. And he wound up also being married to whom? Leah. Now, here's a question. Although a deceiver and being deceived, why did Jacob honor his commitment? There's a principle in scripture as we follow the Spirit that is called integrity. It's the Covenant, which is tied to integrity.

    Let's look at a couple of scriptures that reinforce it.

LESSON 3:
JACOB'S BATTLE OF THE FLESH, EXPERIENCE OF VICTORY OVER THE FLESH, GOD'S FAITHFULNESS DESPITE THE FLESH

> **Read 1 Kings 9:1–9:**
>
> The Lord Appears to Solomon
> **9** As soon as Solomon had finished building the house of the Lord and the king's house and all that Solomon desired to build, ² the Lord appeared to Solomon a second time, as he had appeared to him at Gibeon. ³ And the Lord said to him, "I have heard your prayer and your plea, which you have made before me. I have consecrated this house that you have built, by putting my name there forever. My eyes and my heart will be there for all time. ⁴ And as for you, if you will walk before me, as David your father walked, with integrity of heart and uprightness, doing according to all that I have commanded you, and keeping my statutes and my rules, ⁵ then I will establish your royal throne over Israel forever, as I promised David your father, saying, 'You shall not lack a man on the throne of Israel.' ⁶ But if you turn aside from following me, you or your children, and do not keep my commandments and my statutes that I have set before you, but go and serve other gods and worship them, ⁷ then I will cut off Israel from the land that I have given them, and the house that I have consecrated for my name I will cast out of my sight, and Israel will become a proverb and a byword among all peoples. ⁸ And this house will become a heap of ruins.[a] Everyone passing by it will be astonished and will hiss, and they will say, 'Why has the Lord done thus to this land and to this house?' ⁹ Then they will say, 'Because they abandoned the Lord their God who brought their fathers out of the land of Egypt and laid hold on other gods and worshiped them and served them. Therefore, the Lord has brought all this disaster on them.'"

_____
_____
_____
_____
_____

So, He says, David, who walked with integrity of heart, followed through with what he said. Whatever we say and commit to, we are to follow through on our spoken actions.

LESSON 3:
JACOB'S BATTLE OF THE FLESH, EXPERIENCE OF VICTORY OVER THE FLESH, GOD'S FAITHFULNESS DESPITE THE FLESH

> **Read Proverbs 10:9–11:**
>
> [9] Whoever walks in integrity walks securely,
>   but he who makes his ways crooked will be found out.
> [10] Whoever winks the eye causes trouble,
>   and a babbling fool will come to ruin.
> [11] The mouth of the righteous is a fountain of life,
>   but the mouth of the wicked conceals violence.

_____
_____
_____
_____
_____

If we walk with integrity, we will walk securely and in safety. Why? We then have confidence we will be living in God's Covenant, where God promises protection, safety, and deliverance. If we live in the flesh where we compromise on integrity, God cannot deliver His Covenant benefits.

> **Read Matthew 5:33–37:**
>
> Oaths
> [33] "Again you have heard that it was said to those of old, 'You shall not swear falsely, but shall perform to the Lord what you have sworn.' [34] But I say to you, Do not take an oath at all, either by heaven, for it is the throne of God, [35] or by the earth, for it is his footstool, or by Jerusalem, for it is the city of the great King. [36] And do not take an oath by your head, for you cannot make one hair white or black. [37] Let what you say be simply 'Yes' or 'No'; anything more than this comes from evil.[a]

_____
_____
_____
_____
_____

LESSON 3:
JACOB'S BATTLE OF THE FLESH, EXPERIENCE OF VICTORY OVER THE FLESH, GOD'S FAITHFULNESS DESPITE THE FLESH

We are to let our yes be yes and our no be no. If you have integrity, honor it as spoken and with follow–through in actions, based upon your instructions from God to proceed on a request or action, or not to proceed. You do not always need to explain. The key is to receive your wisdom and insight about the requests and issues before you that involve your response, answers, and actions by seeking God's clarity. Remember, He said, "I've set before you, life and death, blessing or cursing. Let Me guide you into the things I have for you." So, your direction is to come from the Spirit versus your own decisions in the flesh and then honor what you understand with integrity. If you commit to something, but you do not honor it, what does that say about you? You're not trustworthy. This is all based on what is at the essence of your heart—integrity and trustworthiness, regardless of the cost of your commitment.

Think about what is happening to Jacob here. Remember, he's been a deceiver and is fuzzy about following God versus the flesh. One thing that God is teaching him, as he is being transformed and learning to live in the Spirit, is to have integrity. In essence, God is saying, "Even though you committed to this for seven years, honor it; and even though you were deceived for another seven years, but you committed, still honor it." God will bless you as your character is being transformed. This issue of integrity is primary; and then fewer commitments will be important, creating margin to enjoy the life that God has planned for you, as you fulfill the commitments He sanctions for you. This creates peace and joy!

Read through these verses and describe how this family handles having babies. What does this tell you about the flesh and God's ability to use the decisions and outcomes of the flesh for His purposes? What does that mean for us?

> **Read Genesis 29:31–30:24:**
>
> Jacob's Children
> [31] When the Lord saw that Leah was hated, he opened her womb, but Rachel was barren. [32] And Leah conceived and bore a son, and she called his name Reuben,[a] for she said, "Because the Lord has looked upon my affliction; for now my husband will love me." [33] She conceived again and bore a son, and said, "Because the Lord has heard that I am hated, he has given me this son also." And she called his name Simeon.[b] [34] Again she conceived and bore a son, and said, "Now this time my husband will be attached to me, because I have borne him three sons." Therefore his name was called Levi.[c] [35] And she conceived again and bore a son, and said, "This time I will praise the Lord." Therefore she called his name Judah.[d] Then she ceased bearing.

LESSON 3:
JACOB'S BATTLE OF THE FLESH, EXPERIENCE OF VICTORY OVER THE FLESH, GOD'S FAITHFULNESS DESPITE THE FLESH

30 When Rachel saw that she bore Jacob no children, she envied her sister. She said to Jacob, "Give me children, or I shall die!" **2** Jacob's anger was kindled against Rachel, and he said, "Am I in the place of God, who has withheld from you the fruit of the womb?" **3** Then she said, "Here is my servant Bilhah; go in to her, so that she may give birth on my behalf,[e] that even I may have children[f] through her." **4** So she gave him her servant Bilhah as a wife, and Jacob went in to her. **5** And Bilhah conceived and bore Jacob a son. **6** Then Rachel said, "God has judged me, and has also heard my voice and given me a son." Therefore she called his name Dan.[g] **7** Rachel's servant Bilhah conceived again and bore Jacob a second son. **8** Then Rachel said, "With mighty wrestlings[h] I have wrestled with my sister and have prevailed." So she called his name Naphtali.[i]

9 When Leah saw that she had ceased bearing children, she took her servant Zilpah and gave her to Jacob as a wife. **10** Then Leah's servant Zilpah bore Jacob a son. **11** And Leah said, "Good fortune has come!" so she called his name Gad.[j] **12** Leah's servant Zilpah bore Jacob a second son. **13** And Leah said, "Happy am I! For women have called me happy." So she called his name Asher.[k]

14 In the days of wheat harvest Reuben went and found mandrakes in the field and brought them to his mother Leah. Then Rachel said to Leah, "Please give me some of your son's mandrakes." **15** But she said to her, "Is it a small matter that you have taken away my husband? Would you take away my son's mandrakes also?" Rachel said, "Then he may lie with you tonight in exchange for your son's mandrakes." **16** When Jacob came from the field in the evening, Leah went out to meet him and said, "You must come in to me, for I have hired you with my son's mandrakes." So he lay with her that night. **17** And God listened to Leah, and she conceived and bore Jacob a fifth son. **18** Leah said, "God has given me my wages because I gave my servant to my husband." So she called his name Issachar.[l]

19 And Leah conceived again, and she bore Jacob a sixth son. **20** Then Leah said, "God has endowed me with a good endowment; now my husband will honor me, because I have borne him six sons." So she called his name Zebulun.[m] **21** Afterward she bore a daughter and called her name Dinah.

22 Then God remembered Rachel, and God listened to her and opened her womb. **23** She conceived and bore a son and said, "God has taken away my reproach." **24** And she called his name Joseph,[n] saying, "May the Lord add to me another son!"

LESSON 3:
JACOB'S BATTLE OF THE FLESH, EXPERIENCE OF VICTORY OVER THE FLESH, GOD'S FAITHFULNESS DESPITE THE FLESH

_____
_____
_____
_____
_____

What strikes you about this whole thing? Envy, jealousy, manipulation in the flesh on all sides. Leah, Rachel, Jacob. It's all flesh. What is the result? How many sons were born? Twelve. What did they become? They became the 12 tribes of Israel. These 12 tribes of Israel were created and are to be understood as an important part of the spiritual truths throughout all eternity. God's will was to create 12 sons and 12 tribes of Israel. In this situation, did any of them seek God's will? No. They didn't seek God's will. However, God is still going to work through mankind even when those involved are operating in their flesh; it may not be done according to His perfect will, but He still can fulfill His will through His sovereignty. Some examples are:

1. Abraham and Sarah who took things into their own hands and had Abraham lay with Hagar. They had a son, Ishmael, who was not the son of promise and not the offspring that led to the nation of Israel through Isaac and Jacob. Nevertheless, God fulfilled His promise through Abraham putting out the son of the bondwoman and receiving the son of promise, Isaac; God fulfilled His will even though Abraham operated in the flesh.

2. The Israelites who were not willing to go to the promised land because of their self-will, and thus delayed the Israelites going into the promised land and establishing the nation as ordained by God. So, God was angry for 40 years, and waited for 40 years for the next generation to invite them to His will, and established the nation in Israel by occupying the promised land of Canaan. God says that He can still sovereignly fulfill His will, even with our lousy choices.

LESSON 3:
JACOB'S BATTLE OF THE FLESH, EXPERIENCE OF VICTORY OVER THE FLESH, GOD'S FAITHFULNESS DESPITE THE FLESH

Read through these verses and write out the reasons Laban wanted Jacob to stay with him. What did Laban try to do to keep Jacob and/or not have Jacob be blessed? What did God do in this situation? Why? And why is this so significant to us?

Read Genesis 30:25–31:13:

Jacob's Prosperity

25 As soon as Rachel had borne Joseph, Jacob said to Laban, "Send me away, that I may go to my own home and country. 26 Give me my wives and my children for whom I have served you, that I may go, for you know the service that I have given you." 27 But Laban said to him, "If I have found favor in your sight, I have learned by divination that[a] the Lord has blessed me because of you. 28 Name your wages, and I will give it." 29 Jacob said to him, "You yourself know how I have served you, and how your livestock has fared with me. 30 For you had little before I came, and it has increased abundantly, and the Lord has blessed you wherever I turned. But now when shall I provide for my own household also?" 31 He said, "What shall I give you?" Jacob said, "You shall not give me anything. If you will do this for me, I will again pasture your flock and keep it: 32 let me pass through all your flock today, removing from it every speckled and spotted sheep and every black lamb, and the spotted and speckled among the goats, and they shall be my wages. 33 So my honesty will answer for me later, when you come to look into my wages with you. Every one that is not speckled and spotted among the goats and black among the lambs, if found with me, shall be counted stolen." 34 Laban said, "Good! Let it be as you have said." 35 But that day Laban removed the male goats that were striped and spotted, and all the female goats that were speckled and spotted, every one that had white on it, and every lamb that was black, and put them in the charge of his sons. 36 And he set a distance of three days' journey between himself and Jacob, and Jacob pastured the rest of Laban's flock.

37 Then Jacob took fresh sticks of poplar and almond and plane trees, and peeled white streaks in them, exposing the white of the sticks. 38 He set the sticks that he had peeled in front of the flocks in the troughs, that is, the watering places, where the flocks came to drink. And since they bred when they came to drink, 39 the flocks bred in front of the sticks and so the flocks brought forth striped, speckled, and spotted. 40 And Jacob separated the lambs and set the faces of the flocks toward the striped and all the black in the flock of Laban. He put his own droves apart and did not put them with Laban's

LESSON 3:
JACOB'S BATTLE OF THE FLESH, EXPERIENCE OF VICTORY OVER THE FLESH, GOD'S FAITHFULNESS DESPITE THE FLESH

flock. 41 Whenever the stronger of the flock were breeding, Jacob would lay the sticks in the troughs before the eyes of the flock, that they might breed among the sticks, 42 but for the feebler of the flock he would not lay them there. So the feebler would be Laban's, and the stronger Jacob's. 43 Thus the man increased greatly and had large flocks, female servants and male servants, and camels and donkeys.

Jacob Flees from Laban

31 Now Jacob heard that the sons of Laban were saying, "Jacob has taken all that was our father's, and from what was our father's he has gained all this wealth." 2 And Jacob saw that Laban did not regard him with favor as before. 3 Then the Lord said to Jacob, "Return to the land of your fathers and to your kindred, and I will be with you."

4 So Jacob sent and called Rachel and Leah into the field where his flock was 5 and said to them, "I see that your father does not regard me with favor as he did before. But the God of my father has been with me. 6 You know that I have served your father with all my strength, 7 yet your father has cheated me and changed my wages ten times. But God did not permit him to harm me. 8 If he said, 'The spotted shall be your wages,' then all the flock bore spotted; and if he said, 'The striped shall be your wages,' then all the flock bore striped. 9 Thus God has taken away the livestock of your father and given them to me. 10 In the breeding season of the flock I lifted up my eyes and saw in a dream that the goats that mated with the flock were striped, spotted, and mottled. 11 Then the angel of God said to me in the dream, 'Jacob,' and I said, 'Here I am!' 12 And he said, 'Lift up your eyes and see, all the goats that mate with the flock are striped, spotted, and mottled, for I have seen all that Laban is doing to you. 13 I am the God of Bethel, where you anointed a pillar and made a vow to me. Now arise, go out from this land and return to the land of your kindred.'"

_____
_____
_____
_____
_____

LESSON 3:
JACOB'S BATTLE OF THE FLESH, EXPERIENCE OF VICTORY OVER THE FLESH, GOD'S FAITHFULNESS DESPITE THE FLESH

Why did Laban want Jacob to stay with them? He knew God was with Jacob and that he was being blessed because of Jacob. Jacob was multiplying Laban's estate. Laban said to Jacob, "You're really good at this, and I see that God's really blessing you. So, I want you to stay." We can understand this in light of the Covenant. God blesses those who bless you and curses those who curse you. So basically, those who are next to you, who receive and accept you, they are blessings by association. Why did Jacob make the deal? He was learning integrity, a key element of the character of God in which Jacob was to be transformed from deceiver to a follower of God in the Spirit. God had told Jacob to go back to his land. This illustrates the life of God and His will for us. Jacob knew the promise and instruction from God, and did not fret about the timing, or determine his own steps to fulfill God's will. Since returning was going to happen, he knew that as he walked in the will of God, he would continue to be blessed, even though it might not be his own thoughts about the how or when.

What's the trick that Laban tried to play? He tried to hide the sheep that Jacob said he wanted to take. Why? He didn't trust God. He was taking things into his own hands, acting without honor and integrity—completely selfish. And as things played out, he continued to change the rules to gain the advantage for himself. He was totally in the flesh. Nevertheless, God performed the supernatural for Jacob so that despite Laban's trickery, Jacob received the stronger flocks and became exceedingly prosperous (over-the-top blessed). With Jacob learning integrity and how to trust God's will (you will be going home), and listened to God's instructions to him (follow Me and I will lead you through all this, despite the self-centeredness of those around you), he experienced God's will—learning that walking in the Spirit is much more enjoyable and fruitful than walking in the flesh. What does Jacob learn? When you're in dialogue with God, He's removing the fear that triggers you to take things into your own hands, your own will. Rather you're learning to trust God, by learning to hear God and follow God (into the best and none better). Further, you are learning that there is always God's bigger story. God's purposes are not just about us, but about others to whom are in our life and in God's heart. In this case, God is thinking about Laban as well as Jacob. He wanted Laban to experience God's mighty work and see that it was God's mighty work.

LESSON 3:
JACOB'S BATTLE OF THE FLESH, EXPERIENCE OF VICTORY OVER THE FLESH, GOD'S FAITHFULNESS DESPITE THE FLESH

Read through these verses and write down what Jacob did by leaving Laban. What caused him to operate this way, and how did God intervene to fulfill His purposes? Why is this so significant to us?

> **Read Genesis 31:14–55:**
>
> [14] Then Rachel and Leah answered and said to him, "Is there any portion or inheritance left to us in our father's house? [15] Are we not regarded by him as foreigners? For he has sold us, and he has indeed devoured our money. [16] All the wealth that God has taken away from our father belongs to us and to our children. Now then, whatever God has said to you, do."
>
> [17] So Jacob arose and set his sons and his wives on camels. [18] He drove away all his livestock, all his property that he had gained, the livestock in his possession that he had acquired in Paddan-aram, to go to the land of Canaan to his father Isaac. [19] Laban had gone to shear his sheep, and Rachel stole her father's household gods. [20] And Jacob tricked[a] Laban the Aramean, by not telling him that he intended to flee. [21] He fled with all that he had and arose and crossed the Euphrates,[b] and set his face toward the hill country of Gilead.
>
> [22] When it was told Laban on the third day that Jacob had fled, [23] he took his kinsmen with him and pursued him for seven days and followed close after him into the hill country of Gilead. [24] But God came to Laban the Aramean in a dream by night and said to him, "Be careful not to say anything to Jacob, either good or bad."
>
> [25] And Laban overtook Jacob. Now Jacob had pitched his tent in the hill country, and Laban with his kinsmen pitched tents in the hill country of Gilead. [26] And Laban said to Jacob, "What have you done, that you have tricked me and driven away my daughters like captives of the sword? [27] Why did you flee secretly and trick me, and did not tell me, so that I might have sent you away with mirth and songs, with tambourine and lyre? [28] And why did you not permit me to kiss my sons and my daughters farewell? Now you have done foolishly. [29] It is in my power to do you harm. But the God of your[c] father spoke to me last night, saying, 'Be careful not to say anything to Jacob, either good or bad.' [30] And now you have gone away because you longed greatly for your father's house, but why did you steal my gods?" [31] Jacob answered and said to Laban, "Because I was afraid, for I thought that you would take your daughters from me by force. [32] Anyone with whom you find your gods shall not live. In the presence of our kinsmen point out what I have that is yours, and take it." Now Jacob did not know that Rachel had stolen them.

LESSON 3:
JACOB'S BATTLE OF THE FLESH, EXPERIENCE OF VICTORY OVER THE FLESH, GOD'S FAITHFULNESS DESPITE THE FLESH

33 So Laban went into Jacob's tent and into Leah's tent and into the tent of the two female servants, but he did not find them. And he went out of Leah's tent and entered Rachel's. 34 Now Rachel had taken the household gods and put them in the camel's saddle and sat on them. Laban felt all about the tent, but did not find them. 35 And she said to her father, "Let not my lord be angry that I cannot rise before you, for the way of women is upon me." So he searched but did not find the household gods.

36 Then Jacob became angry and berated Laban. Jacob said to Laban, "What is my offense? What is my sin, that you have hotly pursued me? 37 For you have felt through all my goods; what have you found of all your household goods? Set it here before my kinsmen and your kinsmen, that they may decide between us two. 38 These twenty years I have been with you. Your ewes and your female goats have not miscarried, and I have not eaten the rams of your flocks. 39 What was torn by wild beasts I did not bring to you. I bore the loss of it myself. From my hand you required it, whether stolen by day or stolen by night. 40 There I was: by day the heat consumed me, and the cold by night, and my sleep fled from my eyes. 41 These twenty years I have been in your house. I served you fourteen years for your two daughters, and six years for your flock, and you have changed my wages ten times. 42 If the God of my father, the God of Abraham and the Fear of Isaac, had not been on my side, surely now you would have sent me away empty-handed. God saw my affliction and the labor of my hands and rebuked you last night."

43 Then Laban answered and said to Jacob, "The daughters are my daughters, the children are my children, the flocks are my flocks, and all that you see is mine. But what can I do this day for these my daughters or for their children whom they have borne? 44 Come now, let us make a covenant, you and I. And let it be a witness between you and me." 45 So Jacob took a stone and set it up as a pillar. 46 And Jacob said to his kinsmen, "Gather stones." And they took stones and made a heap, and they ate there by the heap. 47 Laban called it Jegar-sahadutha,[d] but Jacob called it Galeed.[e] 48 Laban said, "This heap is a witness between you and me today." Therefore he named it Galeed, 49 and Mizpah,[f] for he said, "The Lord watch between you and me, when we are out of one another's sight. 50 If you oppress my daughters, or if you take wives besides my daughters, although no one is with us, see, God is witness between you and me."

LESSON 3:
JACOB'S BATTLE OF THE FLESH, EXPERIENCE OF VICTORY OVER THE FLESH, GOD'S FAITHFULNESS DESPITE THE FLESH

> ⁵¹ Then Laban said to Jacob, "See this heap and the pillar, which I have set between you and me. ⁵² This heap is a witness, and the pillar is a witness, that I will not pass over this heap to you, and you will not pass over this heap and this pillar to me, to do harm. ⁵³ The God of Abraham and the God of Nahor, the God of their father, judge between us." So Jacob swore by the Fear of his father Isaac, ⁵⁴ and Jacob offered a sacrifice in the hill country and called his kinsmen to eat bread. They ate bread and spent the night in the hill country.
>
> ⁵⁵ [g] Early in the morning Laban arose and kissed his grandchildren and his daughters and blessed them. Then Laban departed and returned home.

_____
_____
_____
_____
_____

What a family. God had told Jacob what, as His promise, was His will? Return home. That was His promise. For Jacob to return home. Let's again explore the difference between the flesh and the Spirit. What did Jacob do with that promise and instruction? What did he not do? He decided to take things into his own hands and make all this work with his own decisions.

Jacob said that he was going to deceive Laban and take off at night. He didn't check in with God. He didn't pursue God or His will. He decided: I'm going to fulfill God's promise, and I'm going to deceive Laban. Laban discovers it. And what's Laban's response? I'm going to go get him. He's going after him. What does God then do? He intervenes, and He speaks to Laban and says: Do not do what you're planning to do, it will not go well if you do this. Laban heard it. He understood it. He did chase him down, and basically said that if it were up to him, he'd take everything Jacob had and go home, including his daughters and grandsons. But, because God intervened, he didn't do that.

And so, God said: I am going to fulfill My plan. You didn't ask Me, but I'm going to do it a different way. I'm sending you home. And the outcome of it all was that the two of them did what? They made an agreement. Laban stated that he was willing to let Jacob go. Laban further said: Don't mistreat my daughters, don't have any more wives, and take care of the grandkids. And then he said: I'm going to bless you.

LESSON 3:
JACOB'S BATTLE OF THE FLESH, EXPERIENCE OF VICTORY OVER THE FLESH, GOD'S FAITHFULNESS DESPITE THE FLESH

Think of what happened to Laban, whose character had been a deceiver, trickster, manipulator, and was self-centered. What happened to him? Through his interaction with God, his heart was changed, and he actually sent Jacob off with the blessing. And through the circumstances of what God did, Laban actually blessed Jacob and set up an agreement where both honored their part. The whole thing flipped because God intervened. Of course, it would have been better for everybody if they would have done what God had asked all along. What would have been God's way all along? God, by the way, wanted to get them both in a place of blessing and agreement and favor. That's what His will was. But they didn't do that. They went off in the flesh. What did God do? He intervened.

There could have been another part to the story. Laban could have said: I don't care. I'm going after it anyway, and God would have said: Ok, then I have a revised plan based upon your response. See how it works. God is sovereign and is capable of fulfilling His will even as our responses and circumstances change, including choosing to go in our own flesh and disregarding God's will. The good news is that we do not have to be perfect the whole time. Even with our poor choices, God is at work, intervening, and inviting us to His resolution, His wonderful will for us, and God's bigger story (which in this situation was for Jacob personally, but also for Laban. God invited him to follow His will, and he received a blessing). For Jacob, Laban could have taken everything. But God said, "Because you have a heart to follow Me, let Me guide you to the next place, and I'll protect it. I'll take care of it all because you have a heart to follow." So, does that mean you have to be perfect? No. But, God's plan would have been a lot easier and much more blessed.

As you review Lesson 3 and understand these stories that illustrate the issue of the flesh, which is manipulation, control, jealousy, envy, and trying to figure things out on your own, we find the beauty of God. We just have to have a heart to follow; and not try to be perfect. Continue to stay with Him as He leads us to His best.

Jesus had stated: The angels are going to ascend and descend upon Him and His life, connecting us in the natural with heaven, the spiritual. They have a specific role of bringing the power of God to us, but we need to understand that they are not God, though they are following the instruction and direction of God (Christ, Jacob's Ladder). Then He gives us an admonition: Do not neglect so great a salvation (we are experiencing all the power, life, and beauty of the spiritual here on Earth, especially as assisted by angels).

Don't neglect so great an opportunity to live in both places. Your salvation, your holiness, your being made whole, your deliverance is the fullness of His life given to us, as we experience Jacob's Ladder. He further adds that the Father will bear witness with signs, miracles and wonders, and gifts of the Holy Spirit, according to His will. The Greek here is the same word: miracles, more and more miracles and the gifts of the Holy Spirit. All the things that He's going to do for

LESSON 3:
JACOB'S BATTLE OF THE FLESH, EXPERIENCE OF VICTORY OVER THE FLESH, GOD'S FAITHFULNESS DESPITE THE FLESH

and through you. God's going to bear witness that there's a connectivity between heaven and Earth. By what? The supernatural. Don't neglect that; don't stop pursuing that. Are you going to live in the Spirit or live in the flesh? Neglecting a great salvation is going the way of Esau. Are you going to live the natural life, missing out on the Covenant life that He wants to give you, which is the supernatural? God will make it real—by connecting Jacob's Ladder, which Jacob got the privilege of seeing right up front. That's why Jacob's Ladder is so critical. It's not just an interesting story. It's a very powerful statement about the life of walking in the Spirit. So, as we finish with Lesson 3, we see further the difference between the flesh and the life of the Spirit with a heart to follow God who will reveal and manifest Himself in the spiritual realm with supernatural things.

With the Covenant, He is going to bless you to make you a blessing.

LESSON 4: JACOB'S WRESTLING WITH GOD AS HE UNDERSTANDS SURRENDER; ISRAEL'S CONTINUED BATTLE WITH THE FLESH/ THE ENEMY (ESAU'S DESCENDANTS)

In Lesson 4, we're going to continue this discussion of the battle of the Spirit versus the flesh and look further at Jacob's life. We have plenty of examples of operating in the flesh, as we've learned, because there's a fundamental issue that Paul states in Romans: Because of the default position of our nature, we go to self. And no matter what we try to do, even good things, we can't fulfill it on our own. And we're in a struggle with God; we're at enmity against God. We put to death the Spirit and cannot please Him as a believer who's operating in the flesh. And we're seeing great examples in the story of Jacob with Laban and all of the situations where they're trying to figure things out and trying to make things happen on their own, in the flesh. But the good news, as we've seen in this last lesson, is that God can intervene through that and continues to say: Well, how about now? Are you willing to follow Me now and let Me keep guiding you? It's not about perfection. It's really about the heart. It would be better if you'd keep seeking Him because He has the better answers.

Now, we're going to get into some more of this story.

> "Because of the default position of our nature, we go to self. And no matter what we try to do, even good things, we can't fulfill it on our own."

Read through these verses and write out how Jacob approached meeting Esau. Why did he operate this way? What actually happened in Jacob's encounter with God? What did this show Jacob and thus, what is the importance to how we live?

> **Read Genesis 32:1–33:19:**
>
> Jacob Fears Esau
> **32** Jacob went on his way, and the angels of God met him. ² And when Jacob saw them he said, "This is God's camp!" So he called the name of that place Mahanaim.[a]
>
> ³ And Jacob sent[b] messengers before him to Esau his brother in the land of Seir, the country of Edom, ⁴ instructing them, "Thus you shall say to my lord Esau: Thus says your servant Jacob, 'I have sojourned with Laban and stayed until now. ⁵ I have oxen, donkeys, flocks, male servants, and female servants. I have sent to tell my lord, in order that I may find favor in your sight.'"

LESSON 4: JACOB'S WRESTLING WITH GOD AS HE UNDERSTANDS SURRENDER; ISRAEL'S CONTINUED BATTLE WITH THE FLESH/ THE ENEMY (ESAU'S DESCENDANTS)

6 And the messengers returned to Jacob, saying, "We came to your brother Esau, and he is coming to meet you, and there are four hundred men with him." 7 Then Jacob was greatly afraid and distressed. He divided the people who were with him, and the flocks and herds and camels, into two camps, 8 thinking, "If Esau comes to the one camp and attacks it, then the camp that is left will escape."

9 And Jacob said, "O God of my father Abraham and God of my father Isaac, O Lord who said to me, 'Return to your country and to your kindred, that I may do you good,' 10 I am not worthy of the least of all the deeds of steadfast love and all the faithfulness that you have shown to your servant, for with only my staff I crossed this Jordan, and now I have become two camps. 11 Please deliver me from the hand of my brother, from the hand of Esau, for I fear him, that he may come and attack me, the mothers with the children. 12 But you said, 'I will surely do you good, and make your offspring as the sand of the sea, which cannot be numbered for multitude.'"

13 So he stayed there that night, and from what he had with him he took a present for his brother Esau, 14 two hundred female goats and twenty male goats, two hundred ewes and twenty rams, 15 thirty milking camels and their calves, forty cows and ten bulls, twenty female donkeys and ten male donkeys. 16 These he handed over to his servants, every drove by itself, and said to his servants, "Pass on ahead of me and put a space between drove and drove." 17 He instructed the first, "When Esau my brother meets you and asks you, 'To whom do you belong? Where are you going? And whose are these ahead of you?' 18 then you shall say, 'They belong to your servant Jacob. They are a present sent to my lord Esau. And moreover, he is behind us.'" 19 He likewise instructed the second and the third and all who followed the droves, "You shall say the same thing to Esau when you find him, 20 and you shall say, 'Moreover, your servant Jacob is behind us.'" For he thought, "I may appease him[c] with the present that goes ahead of me, and afterward I shall see his face. Perhaps he will accept me."[d] 21 So the present passed on ahead of him, and he himself stayed that night in the camp.

Jacob Wrestles with God
22 The same night he arose and took his two wives, his two female servants, and his eleven children,[e] and crossed the ford of the Jabbok. 23 He took them and sent them across the stream, and everything else that he had. 24 And Jacob was left alone. And a man wrestled with him until the breaking of the day. 25 When

LESSON 4: JACOB'S WRESTLING WITH GOD AS HE UNDERSTANDS SURRENDER; ISRAEL'S CONTINUED BATTLE WITH THE FLESH/ THE ENEMY (ESAU'S DESCENDANTS)

the man saw that he did not prevail against Jacob, he touched his hip socket, and Jacob's hip was put out of joint as he wrestled with him. 26 Then he said, "Let me go, for the day has broken." But Jacob said, "I will not let you go unless you bless me." 27 And he said to him, "What is your name?" And he said, "Jacob." 28 Then he said, "Your name shall no longer be called Jacob, but Israel,[f] for you have striven with God and with men, and have prevailed." 29 Then Jacob asked him, "Please tell me your name." But he said, "Why is it that you ask my name?" And there he blessed him. 30 So Jacob called the name of the place Peniel,[g] saying, "For I have seen God face to face, and yet my life has been delivered." 31 The sun rose upon him as he passed Penuel, limping because of his hip. 32 Therefore to this day the people of Israel do not eat the sinew of the thigh that is on the hip socket, because he touched the socket of Jacob's hip on the sinew of the thigh.

Jacob Meets Esau
33 And Jacob lifted up his eyes and looked, and behold, Esau was coming, and four hundred men with him. So he divided the children among Leah and Rachel and the two female servants. 2 And he put the servants with their children in front, then Leah with her children, and Rachel and Joseph last of all. 3 He himself went on before them, bowing himself to the ground seven times, until he came near to his brother.

4 But Esau ran to meet him and embraced him and fell on his neck and kissed him, and they wept. 5 And when Esau lifted up his eyes and saw the women and children, he said, "Who are these with you?" Jacob said, "The children whom God has graciously given your servant." 6 Then the servants drew near, they and their children, and bowed down. 7 Leah likewise and her children drew near and bowed down. And last Joseph and Rachel drew near, and they bowed down. 8 Esau said, "What do you mean by all this company[h] that I met?" Jacob answered, "To find favor in the sight of my lord." 9 But Esau said, "I have enough, my brother; keep what you have for yourself." 10 Jacob said, "No, please, if I have found favor in your sight, then accept my present from my hand. For I have seen your face, which is like seeing the face of God, and you have accepted me. 11 Please accept my blessing that is brought to you, because God has dealt graciously with me, and because I have enough." Thus he urged him, and he took it.

12 Then Esau said, "Let us journey on our way, and I will go ahead of[i] you." 13 But Jacob said to him, "My lord knows that the children are frail, and that the nursing flocks and herds are a care to me. If they are driven hard for one day, all the flocks will die. 14 Let my lord pass on ahead of his servant, and I will lead on slowly, at the pace of the livestock that are ahead of me and at the pace of the children, until I come to my lord in Seir."

LESSON 4: JACOB'S WRESTLING WITH GOD AS HE UNDERSTANDS SURRENDER; ISRAEL'S CONTINUED BATTLE WITH THE FLESH/ THE ENEMY (ESAU'S DESCENDANTS)

> [15] So Esau said, "Let me leave with you some of the people who are with me." But he said, "What need is there? Let me find favor in the sight of my lord." [16] So Esau returned that day on his way to Seir. [17] But Jacob journeyed to Succoth, and built himself a house and made booths for his livestock. Therefore the name of the place is called Succoth.[j]
>
> [18] And Jacob came safely[k] to the city of Shechem, which is in the land of Canaan, on his way from Paddan-aram, and he camped before the city. [19] And from the sons of Hamor, Shechem's father, he bought for a hundred pieces of money[l] the piece of land on which he had pitched his tent.

_____
_____
_____
_____
_____

Jacob is going back home, and who does he expect to meet? Esau. Why? Jacob has taken his birthright, and he is expecting Esau to harm him. Why? What was the last thing he heard from his mom before he left? "Your brother's going to kill you." That's why he had to leave. So, he followed God's instructions and was being obedient about going back home, but as he did, he remembered that Esau was going to try to kill him. And when Esau finds out he's coming back, the first person Jacob is going to meet is him. And, he won't be alone. He will come with others. Four hundred men. Jacob is pretty sure this could be a problem. So, what does Jacob do? He basically gets a bunch of gifts together and launches his own plan. Is he operating in the Spirit or the flesh? He's in the flesh. What's the definition of operating in the flesh? Not checking in, doing your own thing, deciding on your own, "I will." Jacob had planned to give him multiple gifts and keep his distance until he sees how Esau is going to respond. In the first group with all these gifts, he'll likely confiscate everything and go to the second group. He'll do the same there, and then to the third and those following, he'll do the same. Jacob thought that by the time he gets to him, Esau will have softened up because of all the gifts given to him. Isn't this a good idea? There was no processing with God, and with certainty, Jacob had pre-determined that Esau was going to attempt to kill him. He still thinks that he knows what's going to happen, so he makes two mistakes. He presumes what he thinks is possible in the outcome and based upon that, he acts upon his own will, his own plan.

LESSON 4: JACOB'S WRESTLING WITH GOD AS HE UNDERSTANDS SURRENDER; ISRAEL'S CONTINUED BATTLE WITH THE FLESH/ THE ENEMY (ESAU'S DESCENDANTS)

Do you see how you do that? You look at your circumstances, you look at your situation, you look at your decision, you look at the issue, and you conclude, I think it's probably going to look like "this." And since it's going to look like this, let me figure this out based upon my assumption, based upon my action.

While Jacob was preparing to meet Esau, what happened? There was an event with an angel or perhaps even Christ. He engages in wrestling (struggling) with God. What was the wrestling all about? Operating in the flesh versus the Spirit. Was he going to continue making decisions on his own, in the flesh, or was he going to surrender to the will and direction of God?

God is saying, "Are you going to follow Me or not? You have a heart to, and you've been listening somewhat to Me, but the truth is, your heart isn't really surrendered. This is evidenced by you continuing to try to figure things out on your own." And He keeps saying to Jacob, "You don't get this yet. So, we're going to wrestle all night." What is the wrestling all about? Surrender. It is a struggle. It's a battle. And it is wrestling because it can't happen in the head. It has to happen in the heart. It has to happen at the soul level. Jesus did the same thing when He went to the Garden of Gethsemane. He spent an hour or so and wrestled, and it even says in Mark, "Father, You are sovereign. And I know Your sovereignty, creativity, ability to change things, make things happen. You can do this differently." He walks out of the garden and says, "Not My will be done but Yours." But why did He go back in? Because it wasn't settled. He said, "I know I'm supposed to surrender. But the truth is, I'm not surrendered. It is in My head but not My heart." So, He goes back in and says the same thing, "Let this cup pass from Me." This goes on for another hour or so. He struggled. And again, He wrestled. "Not My will be done but Yours." Why did He go back in the third time? He had to wrestle some more. He didn't have it yet, so He goes back in the third time, and it got so intense that His blood vessels in His forehead burst. Think about how intense that must have been. And then He comes out and says, "It's settled. I've wrestled through the process of getting it settled. I'm ready to go." Did He ever struggle again with that issue? No. He conquered the self. Paul writes about this in Romans Chapter 5: By one man (His creation—Adam and Eve, one man and woman), sin came into the world by what: exercising free will in the self versus in the Spirit. But this was overcome by Jesus's struggle with self–will, and He overcame it at the Garden of Gethsemane.

So, it was this place of struggle with the will to surrender and then putting to death that struggle. That's why Jesus told us the key to everyday living and how to overcome the sin nature of flesh/self and follow Him: "Deny self (struggle) and surrender. Take up the cross, stand on what I've done, and put to death the flesh." And then what are we to do? "Come and follow". We are to spend our time following Christ and receiving the life He has for you."—and this is required all

LESSON 4: JACOB'S WRESTLING WITH GOD AS HE UNDERSTANDS SURRENDER; ISRAEL'S CONTINUED BATTLE WITH THE FLESH/ THE ENEMY (ESAU'S DESCENDANTS)

the time, every single day and every moment—is not once for all, but a continual process of denying self and following Him.

Here, Jacob is wrestling all night, and Jesus said He'd end it. But Jacob said, "No." What else did he say? "I will not release this until you bless me." That's the surrender. He was not going to quit too early until he got the blessing. And what's the blessing? A heart that was willing to follow Him, which is best and none better. Know and see what God is doing. He was testing him. Jacob wrestled all night, but he was not there yet. Did he want to give up? To quit? And to Jacob's credit, he said, "No." He was going to stay until it got resolved. And he got it resolved.

It's two parts: It's surrendering your rulership over your own life and what you want to do; and then surrendering it to the point where you're willing to follow Him completely.

Another interesting part of the story: Jacob's hip was dislocated. Why? So, he could remember. He could remember what he did, how he surrendered. "And I'm going to give you a physical representation of surrender and change your name from Jacob, who's a deceiver, to Israel, who is a follower of God." What a significant truth: When you surrender and decide to follow, your life is now living in the Spirit, being led by God into His will. You no longer will be hampered by your flesh and your patterns (like Jacob being a deceiver) but will now be a true follower.

It's also interesting that after he's done wrestling and he's surrendered, God says that Jacob has strived with God and men and has prevailed. Once you have surrendered, you've actually prevailed.

Read through these sets of verses and write out how and why we are to "wrestle things out with God." Why is this so important and a requirement for living in the Spirit versus the flesh?

> **Read John 4:34:**
>
> ³⁴ Jesus said to them, "My food is to do the will of him who sent me and to accomplish his work.

_____
_____
_____
_____
_____

LESSON 4: JACOB'S WRESTLING WITH GOD AS HE UNDERSTANDS SURRENDER; ISRAEL'S CONTINUED BATTLE WITH THE FLESH/ THE ENEMY (ESAU'S DESCENDANTS)

> **Read John 6:38:**
>
> [38] For I have come down from heaven, not to do my own will but the will of him who sent me.

_____
_____
_____
_____

Jesus makes it very clear His purpose is to do what? To do the will of the Father. Remember who's living within us? Christ. As Christ lived, so are we to live, as He is living His life through us. He only does the will of the Father. He surrendered His will, including the ultimate challenge of going to His death and fighting through to complete surrender.

> **Read John 10:17–18:**
>
> [17] For this reason the Father loves me, because I lay down my life that I may take it up again. [18] No one takes it from me, but I lay it down of my own accord. I have authority to lay it down, and I have authority to take it up again. This charge I have received from my Father."

_____
_____
_____
_____

Jesus tells us: I'm going to go to My death, and the Father is not going to assist Me. He gives Me the power to fulfill all else, but this point of My complete surrender to go to the cross is completely My battle—conquering self.

LESSON 4: JACOB'S WRESTLING WITH GOD AS HE UNDERSTANDS SURRENDER; ISRAEL'S CONTINUED BATTLE WITH THE FLESH/ THE ENEMY (ESAU'S DESCENDANTS)

> **Read John 15:1–8:**
>
> I Am the True Vine
> **15** "I am the true vine, and my Father is the vinedresser. ² Every branch in me that does not bear fruit he takes away, and every branch that does bear fruit he prunes, that it may bear more fruit. ³ Already you are clean because of the word that I have spoken to you. ⁴ Abide in me, and I in you. As the branch cannot bear fruit by itself, unless it abides in the vine, neither can you, unless you abide in me. ⁵ I am the vine; you are the branches. Whoever abides in me and I in him, he it is that bears much fruit, for apart from me you can do nothing. ⁶ If anyone does not abide in me he is thrown away like a branch and withers; and the branches are gathered, thrown into the fire, and burned. ⁷ If you abide in me, and my words abide in you, ask whatever you wish, and it will be done for you. ⁸ By this my Father is glorified, that you bear much fruit and so prove to be my disciples.

_____
_____
_____
_____
_____

    This is Christ's analogy of the vine and vineyard: abiding in Him. Living Waters has a whole course on this: Abiding in the Vine. In unity, work through what it means to surrender, abide in the relationship, walk with Him, and experience His abundant life for us. Jesus states: I'm the vine, the Father's the vine dresser. You are the branches. Abide with Me. Stay connected to Me. Your choice is to stay connected to Me. And then He makes this statement: Apart from Me, you can do what? Nothing. And He makes that emphatic. If you don't abide with Me, everything you do is worthless, and it's going to be burned up. Which, by the way, Paul reiterates in 1 Corinthians 3: You could be a believer and your whole life has burned up as if nothing. Jesus says: When I came, I demonstrated following the will of God. I'm going to transfer that to you in order for you to live the life of God. What do you have to do? Follow God's will.

    If you are not following God's will, you're doing nothing. If you follow Him and you abide in Him, you receive His will and not your own plan, which will not allow

LESSON 4: JACOB'S WRESTLING WITH GOD AS HE UNDERSTANDS SURRENDER; ISRAEL'S CONTINUED BATTLE WITH THE FLESH/ THE ENEMY (ESAU'S DESCENDANTS)

Him to deliver to you the Covenant life, the abundant life, best and none better. His will is received through your abiding, and you will receive His Word, His promises, His truth. You can then pray it, and it'll happen. And the Father will be glorified. The supernatural is going to happen. Fantastic stuff is going to happen. Apart from Him, you can do nothing. So, He transfers that to you, and you're going to have to wrestle through like Jacob. And then it will be made clear if you are really surrendered.

When Jacob had the problem with Laban, God told him, "I've got this." He expressed His will, and Jacob heard His will. He was learning to hear His will. This is the essence of abiding: surrendering and being willing to learn to hear and follow His will. We do not need to be perfect, just have a heart to follow and stay connected.

So, as God was teaching Jacob how to surrender and abide, he experiences a different path than he thought was possible with Esau. What actually happened? Esau came and greeted him with a desire to rebuild the relationship, to reconcile. "Welcome back. No, I'm not going to kill you. I will actually protect you. You don't need to give me all this stuff. You're my brother. Welcome home, let me help you." What would have been easier for Jacob to have done originally? Just ask God what was going to happen. Jacob was planning based upon his own logic and was operating in fear. He did not fully understand and receive the Covenant—to be blessed to be a blessing.

In this situation, it does not negate that Esau is still operating in the flesh. Though for the moment, there is reconciliation and the welcoming of rebuilding the relationship, the path ahead has difficulty because of Esau's selfishness and not following God's will.

Read through these verses and write out the promise given to Jacob and the significance to us as believers. What is God's story that is being revealed, and why is it so significant to us?

> **Read Genesis 35:1–36:13:**
>
> God Blesses and Renames Jacob
> **35** God said to Jacob, "Arise, go up to Bethel and dwell there. Make an altar there to the God who appeared to you when you fled from your brother Esau." ² So Jacob said to his household and to all who were with him, "Put away the foreign gods that are among you and purify yourselves and change your garments. ³ Then let us arise and go up to Bethel, so that I may make there an altar to the God who answers me in the day of my distress and has been with me wherever I have gone." ⁴ So they gave to Jacob all the foreign gods that they

LESSON 4: JACOB'S WRESTLING WITH GOD AS HE UNDERSTANDS SURRENDER; ISRAEL'S CONTINUED BATTLE WITH THE FLESH/ THE ENEMY (ESAU'S DESCENDANTS)

had, and the rings that were in their ears. Jacob hid them under the terebinth tree that was near Shechem.

5 And as they journeyed, a terror from God fell upon the cities that were around them, so that they did not pursue the sons of Jacob. 6 And Jacob came to Luz (that is, Bethel), which is in the land of Canaan, he and all the people who were with him, 7 and there he built an altar and called the place El-bethel,[a] because there God had revealed himself to him when he fled from his brother. 8 And Deborah, Rebekah's nurse, died, and she was buried under an oak below Bethel. So he called its name Allon-bacuth.[b]

9 God appeared[c] to Jacob again, when he came from Paddan-aram, and blessed him. 10 And God said to him, "Your name is Jacob; no longer shall your name be called Jacob, but Israel shall be your name." So he called his name Israel. 11 And God said to him, "I am God Almighty:[d] be fruitful and multiply. A nation and a company of nations shall come from you, and kings shall come from your own body.[e] 12 The land that I gave to Abraham and Isaac I will give to you, and I will give the land to your offspring after you." 13 Then God went up from him in the place where he had spoken with him. 14 And Jacob set up a pillar in the place where he had spoken with him, a pillar of stone. He poured out a drink offering on it and poured oil on it. 15 So Jacob called the name of the place where God had spoken with him Bethel.

The Deaths of Rachel and Isaac
16 Then they journeyed from Bethel. When they were still some distance[f] from Ephrath, Rachel went into labor, and she had hard labor. 17 And when her labor was at its hardest, the midwife said to her, "Do not fear, for you have another son." 18 And as her soul was departing (for she was dying), she called his name Ben-oni;[g] but his father called him Benjamin.[h] 19 So Rachel died, and she was buried on the way to Ephrath (that is, Bethlehem), 20 and Jacob set up a pillar over her tomb. It is the pillar of Rachel's tomb, which is there to this day. 21 Israel journeyed on and pitched his tent beyond the tower of Eder.

22 While Israel lived in that land, Reuben went and lay with Bilhah his father's concubine. And Israel heard of it.

Now the sons of Jacob were twelve. 23 The sons of Leah: Reuben (Jacob's firstborn), Simeon, Levi, Judah, Issachar, and Zebulun. 24 The sons of Rachel: Joseph and Benjamin. 25 The sons of Bilhah, Rachel's servant: Dan and Naphtali. 26 The sons of Zilpah, Leah's servant: Gad and Asher. These were the sons of Jacob who were born to him in Paddan-aram.

LESSON 4: JACOB'S WRESTLING WITH GOD AS HE UNDERSTANDS SURRENDER; ISRAEL'S CONTINUED BATTLE WITH THE FLESH/ THE ENEMY (ESAU'S DESCENDANTS)

27 And Jacob came to his father Isaac at Mamre, or Kiriath-arba (that is, Hebron), where Abraham and Isaac had sojourned. 28 Now the days of Isaac were 180 years. 29 And Isaac breathed his last, and he died and was gathered to his people, old and full of days. And his sons Esau and Jacob buried him.

Esau's Descendants
36 These are the generations of Esau (that is, Edom). 2 Esau took his wives from the Canaanites: Adah the daughter of Elon the Hittite, Oholibamah the daughter of Anah the daughter[i] of Zibeon the Hivite, 3 and Basemath, Ishmael's daughter, the sister of Nebaioth. 4 And Adah bore to Esau, Eliphaz; Basemath bore Reuel; 5 and Oholibamah bore Jeush, Jalam, and Korah. These are the sons of Esau who were born to him in the land of Canaan.

6 Then Esau took his wives, his sons, his daughters, and all the members of his household, his livestock, all his beasts, and all his property that he had acquired in the land of Canaan. He went into a land away from his brother Jacob. 7 For their possessions were too great for them to dwell together. The land of their sojournings could not support them because of their livestock. 8 So Esau settled in the hill country of Seir. (Esau is Edom.)

9 These are the generations of Esau the father of the Edomites in the hill country of Seir. 10 These are the names of Esau's sons: Eliphaz the son of Adah the wife of Esau, Reuel the son of Basemath the wife of Esau. 11 The sons of Eliphaz were Teman, Omar, Zepho, Gatam, and Kenaz. 12 (Timna was a concubine of Eliphaz, Esau's son; she bore Amalek to Eliphaz.) These are the sons of Adah, Esau's wife. 13 These are the sons of Reuel: Nahath, Zerah, Shammah, and Mizzah. These are the sons of Basemath, Esau's wife.

LESSON 4: JACOB'S WRESTLING WITH GOD AS HE UNDERSTANDS SURRENDER; ISRAEL'S CONTINUED BATTLE WITH THE FLESH/ THE ENEMY (ESAU'S DESCENDANTS)

What is the significance of all those names?

Bethel is a specific place within the entire land of Canaan. What does that imply? This was the first step in the overall process of occupying this land as God's "Promised land." God promised Abraham and Isaac that they would be established as a nation in this land of Canaan. God's promises were very specific. As He said in John, "If you abide in Me, in My Word, My promises, My statements, you will receive it, own it, and occupy it," which was given to Jacob to begin the settlement, step by step. "The first step is Bethel and ultimately through following each step, he was to occupy the whole land." (Note: Rachel has the 12th son, Benjamin. And he settles in Bethlehem. Who's of the tribe of Benjamin? Jesus, who is the Messiah, which in the broadest sense, is the fullness of the blessing as promised to Abraham.) It says in Micah that the Messiah is going to be born where? Bethlehem. Jacob (Israel) is part of the bigger story. Another interesting truth is that Saul, who became Paul, was of the tribe of Benjamin. The one who writes most of the New Testament is of that tribe as well. More blessing to the world.

In the list all of the offspring of Esau, who's now called Edom (Edomites), one of them is Eliphaz, who produced Amalek (Amalekites), which you will see is significant.

Read through these verses and write out the significance of the Amalekites and how they still impact our lives today. How are we to respond to the enemy? What does this provide for us? Why is this so significant for us?

> **Read Exodus 17:8–16:**
>
> Israel Defeats Amalek
> 8 Then Amalek came and fought with Israel at Rephidim. 9 So Moses said to Joshua, "Choose for us men, and go out and fight with Amalek. Tomorrow I will stand on the top of the hill with the staff of God in my hand." 10 So Joshua did as Moses told him, and fought with Amalek, while Moses, Aaron, and Hur went up to the top of the hill. 11 Whenever Moses held up his hand, Israel prevailed, and whenever he lowered his hand, Amalek prevailed. 12 But Moses' hands grew weary, so they took a stone and put it under him, and he sat on it, while Aaron and Hur held up his hands, one on one side, and the other on the other side. So his hands were steady until the going down of the sun. 13 And Joshua overwhelmed Amalek and his people with the sword.

LESSON 4: JACOB'S WRESTLING WITH GOD AS HE UNDERSTANDS SURRENDER; ISRAEL'S CONTINUED BATTLE WITH THE FLESH/ THE ENEMY (ESAU'S DESCENDANTS)

> [14] Then the Lord said to Moses, "Write this as a memorial in a book and recite it in the ears of Joshua, that I will utterly blot out the memory of Amalek from under heaven." [15] And Moses built an altar and called the name of it, The Lord Is My Banner, [16] saying, "A hand upon the throne[a] of the Lord! The Lord will have war with Amalek from generation to generation."

_____
_____
_____
_____
_____

The Amalekites are descendants of Esau, representing the flesh who are at war with whom? Israel, who is representing the Spirit. Esau is flesh and his offspring is flesh. And guess what? They're at war with those in the Spirit, which Paul says in Galatians. Your flesh is at war with the Spirit, and your Spirit is at war with the flesh. And Exodus states that we, as followers of God, are going to be fighting the Amalekites from generation to generation. In other words, everybody who is a follower of Christ in the Spirit is going to have Amalekites in our lives—people around who are in the flesh and who are coming against the work of God. And, of course, the key is, as stated to Joshua and Moses, you have to address it, to take care of it.

How did Moses prevail through prayer? Through the power of God. God said, "If you stop staying in the Spirit, you're going to get defeated. And because this is difficult to do on your own, get some helpers to strengthen you and keep you strong in that place of the Spirit; and then you'll prevail." Prevail is a great word-picture of staying in the spirit or not. Don't be defeated by the Amalekites who constantly come against you. Don't join them by going to the flesh. They could have been defeated through the spiritual power of God (against any attack or negative circumstance).

This whole story of Israel and walking in the Spirit is beginning to become clear: You need to follow God, listen to God, understand God, and know God's will. You're going to occupy the land. But guess what? There are going to be battles that you're going to have to go through, but God will do the work. But you've got to follow Him. Even though Esau had reconciled with God, he and his offspring still represent the flesh, which will be at enmity against God and against you.

LESSON 4: JACOB'S WRESTLING WITH GOD AS HE UNDERSTANDS SURRENDER; ISRAEL'S CONTINUED BATTLE WITH THE FLESH/ THE ENEMY (ESAU'S DESCENDANTS)

Read through these sets of verses and write out what happened with Balaam. What does this mean for us today?

Read Numbers 22:1–41:

Balak Summons Balaam

22 Then the people of Israel set out and camped in the plains of Moab beyond the Jordan at Jericho. ² And Balak the son of Zippor saw all that Israel had done to the Amorites. ³ And Moab was in great dread of the people, because they were many. Moab was overcome with fear of the people of Israel. ⁴ And Moab said to the elders of Midian, "This horde will now lick up all that is around us, as the ox licks up the grass of the field." So Balak the son of Zippor, who was king of Moab at that time, ⁵ sent messengers to Balaam the son of Beor at Pethor, which is near the River[a] in the land of the people of Amaw,[b] to call him, saying, "Behold, a people has come out of Egypt. They cover the face of the earth, and they are dwelling opposite me. ⁶ Come now, curse this people for me, since they are too mighty for me. Perhaps I shall be able to defeat them and drive them from the land, for I know that he whom you bless is blessed, and he whom you curse is cursed."

⁷ So the elders of Moab and the elders of Midian departed with the fees for divination in their hand. And they came to Balaam and gave him Balak's message. ⁸ And he said to them, "Lodge here tonight, and I will bring back word to you, as the Lord speaks to me." So the princes of Moab stayed with Balaam. ⁹ And God came to Balaam and said, "Who are these men with you?" ¹⁰ And Balaam said to God, "Balak the son of Zippor, king of Moab, has sent to me, saying, ¹¹ 'Behold, a people has come out of Egypt, and it covers the face of the earth. Now come, curse them for me. Perhaps I shall be able to fight against them and drive them out.'" ¹² God said to Balaam, "You shall not go with them. You shall not curse the people, for they are blessed." ¹³ So Balaam rose in the morning and said to the princes of Balak, "Go to your own land, for the Lord has refused to let me go with you." ¹⁴ So the princes of Moab rose and went to Balak and said, "Balaam refuses to come with us."

¹⁵ Once again Balak sent princes, more in number and more honorable than these. ¹⁶ And they came to Balaam and said to him, "Thus says Balak the son of Zippor: 'Let nothing hinder you from coming to me, ¹⁷ for I will surely do you great honor, and whatever you say to me I will do. Come, curse this people for me.'" ¹⁸ But Balaam answered and said to the servants of Balak, "Though Balak were to give me his house full of silver and gold, I could not go beyond the

LESSON 4: JACOB'S WRESTLING WITH GOD AS HE UNDERSTANDS SURRENDER; ISRAEL'S CONTINUED BATTLE WITH THE FLESH/ THE ENEMY (ESAU'S DESCENDANTS)

command of the Lord my God to do less or more. [19] So you, too, please stay here tonight, that I may know what more the Lord will say to me." [20] And God came to Balaam at night and said to him, "If the men have come to call you, rise, go with them; but only do what I tell you." [21] So Balaam rose in the morning and saddled his donkey and went with the princes of Moab.

Balaam's Donkey and the Angel
[22] But God's anger was kindled because he went, and the angel of the Lord took his stand in the way as his adversary. Now he was riding on the donkey, and his two servants were with him. [23] And the donkey saw the angel of the Lord standing in the road, with a drawn sword in his hand. And the donkey turned aside out of the road and went into the field. And Balaam struck the donkey, to turn her into the road. [24] Then the angel of the Lord stood in a narrow path between the vineyards, with a wall on either side. [25] And when the donkey saw the angel of the Lord, she pushed against the wall and pressed Balaam's foot against the wall. So he struck her again. [26] Then the angel of the Lord went ahead and stood in a narrow place, where there was no way to turn either to the right or to the left. [27] When the donkey saw the angel of the Lord, she lay down under Balaam. And Balaam's anger was kindled, and he struck the donkey with his staff. [28] Then the Lord opened the mouth of the donkey, and she said to Balaam, "What have I done to you, that you have struck me these three times?" [29] And Balaam said to the donkey, "Because you have made a fool of me. I wish I had a sword in my hand, for then I would kill you." [30] And the donkey said to Balaam, "Am I not your donkey, on which you have ridden all your life long to this day? Is it my habit to treat you this way?" And he said, "No."

[31] Then the Lord opened the eyes of Balaam, and he saw the angel of the Lord standing in the way, with his drawn sword in his hand. And he bowed down and fell on his face. [32] And the angel of the Lord said to him, "Why have you struck your donkey these three times? Behold, I have come out to oppose you because your way is perverse[c] before me. [33] The donkey saw me and turned aside before me these three times. If she had not turned aside from me, surely just now I would have killed you and let her live." [34] Then Balaam said to the angel of the Lord, "I have sinned, for I did not know that you stood in the road against me. Now therefore, if it is evil in your sight, I will turn back." [35] And the angel of the Lord said to Balaam, "Go with the men, but speak only the word that I tell you." So Balaam went on with the princes of Balak.

LESSON 4: JACOB'S WRESTLING WITH GOD AS HE UNDERSTANDS SURRENDER; ISRAEL'S CONTINUED BATTLE WITH THE FLESH/ THE ENEMY (ESAU'S DESCENDANTS)

> 36 When Balak heard that Balaam had come, he went out to meet him at the city of Moab, on the border formed by the Arnon, at the extremity of the border. 37 And Balak said to Balaam, "Did I not send to you to call you? Why did you not come to me? Am I not able to honor you?" 38 Balaam said to Balak, "Behold, I have come to you! Have I now any power of my own to speak anything? The word that God puts in my mouth, that must I speak." 39 Then Balaam went with Balak, and they came to Kiriath-huzoth. 40 And Balak sacrificed oxen and sheep, and sent for Balaam and for the princes who were with him.
>
> 41 And in the morning Balak took Balaam and brought him up to Bamoth-baal, and from there he saw a fraction of the people.

_____
_____
_____
_____
_____

Read Numbers 23:11–12:

> 11 And Balak said to Balaam, "What have you done to me? I took you to curse my enemies, and behold, you have done nothing but bless them." 12 And he answered and said, "Must I not take care to speak what the Lord puts in my mouth?"

_____
_____
_____
_____
_____

LESSON 4: JACOB'S WRESTLING WITH GOD AS HE UNDERSTANDS SURRENDER; ISRAEL'S CONTINUED BATTLE WITH THE FLESH/ THE ENEMY (ESAU'S DESCENDANTS)

> **Read Numbers 23:25–26:**
>
> [25] And Balak said to Balaam, "Do not curse them at all, and do not bless them at all." [26] But Balaam answered Balak, "Did I not tell you, 'All that the Lord says, that I must do'?"

_____
_____
_____
_____

> **Read Numbers 24:10–14:**
>
> [10] And Balak's anger was kindled against Balaam, and he struck his hands together. And Balak said to Balaam, "I called you to curse my enemies, and behold, you have blessed them these three times. [11] Therefore now flee to your own place. I said, 'I will certainly honor you,' but the Lord has held you back from honor." [12] And Balaam said to Balak, "Did I not tell your messengers whom you sent to me, [13] 'If Balak should give me his house full of silver and gold, I would not be able to go beyond the word of the Lord, to do either good or bad of my own will. What the Lord speaks, that will I speak'? [14] And now, behold, I am going to my people. Come, I will let you know what this people will do to your people in the latter days."

_____
_____
_____
_____
_____

LESSON 4: JACOB'S WRESTLING WITH GOD AS HE UNDERSTANDS SURRENDER; ISRAEL'S CONTINUED BATTLE WITH THE FLESH/ THE ENEMY (ESAU'S DESCENDANTS)

Balak is Moab, who's against Israel—a battle of the flesh against the Spirit. And the flesh is desiring to curse (come against) the Spirit. Why? Fear and wanting to lead a self-centered life instead of surrendering to God's life. You must understand that as a believer, you can be in the place of Balak. You say that you want to be with God, that you'd like to follow God, but you're in the flesh. And God says that what is actually happening is that you are fighting against Him. But it's not only about struggling to follow Him with a true heart to follow, rather, you're actually at enmity against Him. This means you are trying to prevail over anything that God would do because you don't care. The flesh wants to silence what? The Spirit.

But, what happens on Balaam's way? The Angel of the Lord stands in front of them.

Who noticed the angel first? The donkey.

Balaam is mad at his donkey, and the donkey is strangely, yet amazingly talking. The angel finally says, "Fortunately, your donkey saw me. If it were up to me, I would just kill you. You're so disobedient, you deserve to be killed." Then, to Balaam's credit, he repents. He knows he has operated in the flesh. So, you can see the dual problem: The flesh is trying to silence the Spirit, to promote disobedience. Balaam is trying to follow God, but he gets caught up in his own flesh.

What was his disobedience? After all, God told him to go, and he went. Then the Angel of the Lord stopped him on the way, and when all was said and done, Balaam said that God told him not to go again. What really happened? God said something, but He didn't say that. God couldn't say, "Go but then I'm going to kill you for going." That doesn't hold up. Balaam didn't hear God. He put his own spin on what God said. Since God intervened and Balaam understood through the supernatural intervention that he was called to repent, he was then given instruction (now being right with God in the Spirit) to go ahead to speak everything He told him but only what He told him. And to follow God. Now, he's back in the Spirit. The good news about all that is that once he repented and had a heart to follow God, God could reveal a new plan for him.

God's will is always moving us forward, even as He works through the lousy choices we make before choosing a heart to walk in the Spirit and not the flesh.

The whole process of the flesh and the Spirit is realizing that there's a battle, and the flesh wants to silence the Spirit. As you make your decisions, remember the issue you're facing is dealing with the flesh that is trying to prevail over the Spirit. It takes a choice to follow Him and to receive His plan for you, which is to bless you and to make you a blessing to others.

LESSON 5:
HOW WE LIFE IN THE SPIRIT AND EXPERIENCE GOD'S POWER OVER THE FLESH AND THE ENEMY

In Lesson 5, we conclude our study: *The Battle of the Flesh versus the Spirit*. As we have understood, because of what Paul stated and what's true, our default position is to embrace the flesh, which is defined as self, self-determination, self-will. We've seen this through the study of Jacob, who is now called Israel. We also have seen the natural opposition, which is represented by Esau, who is called Edom, and the Edomites and Amalekites. We are caught up in the same battle as Jacob, and we flip back and forth between wanting to follow God, but also wanting to follow our own plan that we hope God will bless. Do we have a heart to follow God's will? Yes. Do you know how to do it? Not really. And therefore, we go back to the flesh, which means we're at enmity against God, and we're trying to silence the Spirit. So, we're going to spend our time in this concluding lesson discovering how to overcome that battle and seek God.

Let's first review Balaam. He let his own flesh get in the way and was disobedient, and it took the angel and Balaam's donkey to redirect him. But, to his credit, what did he do? He repented. Remember, the sin isn't the act in which you are engaged. It's walking in the flesh. It may translate into addiction, fear, anxiety, worry, anger. You can say, "Well, that's the sin." But it's not. It's the fact that you are not following God. Balaam decided just to follow what God had to say. He was no longer going to operate in the flesh but instead, stay in the Spirit and follow God, which ultimately blessed Israel.

> "Remember, the sin isn't the act in which you are engaged. It's walking in the flesh. It may translate into addiction, fear, anxiety, worry, anger."

Read through these verses and write out the principles that we are to receive regarding what was revealed to Balaam and the significance it has to us today.

Read Numbers 24:15–25:

Balaam's Final Oracle
15 And he took up his discourse and said,

"The oracle of Balaam the son of Beor,
  the oracle of the man whose eye is opened,
16 the oracle of him who hears the words of God,
  and knows the knowledge of the Most High,
who sees the vision of the Almighty,

LESSON 5:
HOW WE LIFE IN THE SPIRIT AND EXPERIENCE GOD'S POWER OVER THE FLESH AND THE ENEMY

> falling down with his eyes uncovered:
> ¹⁷ I see him, but not now;
>   I behold him, but not near:
> a star shall come out of Jacob,
>   and a scepter shall rise out of Israel;
> it shall crush the forehead[a] of Moab
>   and break down all the sons of Sheth.
> ¹⁸ Edom shall be dispossessed;
>   Seir also, his enemies, shall be dispossessed.
>   Israel is doing valiantly.
> ¹⁹ And one from Jacob shall exercise dominion
>   and destroy the survivors of cities!"
>
> ²⁰ Then he looked on Amalek and took up his discourse and said,
> "Amalek was the first among the nations,
>   but its end is utter destruction."
>
> ²¹ And he looked on the Kenite, and took up his discourse and said,
> "Enduring is your dwelling place,
>   and your nest is set in the rock.
> ²² Nevertheless, Kain shall be burned
>   when Asshur takes you away captive."
>
> ²³ And he took up his discourse and said,
> "Alas, who shall live when God does this?
> ²⁴ But ships shall come from Kittim
>   and shall afflict Asshur and Eber;
>   and he too shall come to utter destruction."
>
> ²⁵ Then Balaam rose and went back to his place. And Balak also went his way.

_____
_____
_____
_____
_____

He's given a prophecy. As Balaam was speaking the blessing as instructed, God told him that He had something more to reveal to him. This was not even being

LESSON 5:
HOW WE LIFE IN THE SPIRIT AND EXPERIENCE GOD'S POWER OVER THE FLESH AND THE ENEMY

sought by Balaam but rather God intervened and revealed a significant prophetic word that Balaam now had the privilege to receive. God revealed that Jesus, the Messiah, was coming, and the Messiah was going to prevail. At its complete spiritual level, who is God going to prevail over? Who is Jesus going to prevail over? Satan! Because we are going to prevail over the flesh, which is under the control and operation of Satan. Christ is going to crush the head of Satan and have victory, overcoming (prevailing) principalities and powers—disarming them and gaining victory over them.

Read through these sets of verses and write out the basis by which we are protected. How then should we proceed when attacked by the enemy? Why is this so important to us in our everyday lives?

> **Read Colossians 2:11–15:**
>
> ¹¹ In him also you were circumcised with a circumcision made without hands, by putting off the body of the flesh, by the circumcision of Christ, ¹² having been buried with him in baptism, in which you were also raised with him through faith in the powerful working of God, who raised him from the dead. ¹³ And you, who were dead in your trespasses and the uncircumcision of your flesh, God made alive together with him, having forgiven us all our trespasses, ¹⁴ by canceling the record of debt that stood against us with its legal demands. This he set aside, nailing it to the cross. ¹⁵ He disarmed the rulers and authorities[a] and put them to open shame, by triumphing over them in him.[b]

_____
_____
_____
_____
_____

Christ has overcome the enemy. The enemy is disarmed (has no power in the presence and Kingdom of God); and Satan is going to be defeated, victory has been won. There are no longer any battles that need to be fought. Did Satan completely disappear? No. So then, where is the defeat? The heavenly place. It occurs in the heavenly, and it occurs in His Kingdom. Yes, we live in two places at once: the flesh, which is the natural world, and the spiritual, God's Kingdom. Is he defeated in the natural? No, he's still here. So, there's the battle. Do we have the

LESSON 5:
HOW WE LIFE IN THE SPIRIT AND EXPERIENCE GOD'S POWER OVER THE FLESH AND THE ENEMY

power to overcome it? In the natural, the flesh, no, but in the Kingdom, yes. The battle there is over, and Satan has no power and no possibility of victory as this already has been won by Christ.

> **Read Deuteronomy 25:17–19:**
>
> [17] "Remember what Amalek did to you on the way as you came out of Egypt, [18] how he attacked you on the way when you were faint and weary, and cut off your tail, those who were lagging behind you, and he did not fear God. [19] Therefore when the Lord your God has given you rest from all your enemies around you, in the land that the Lord your God is giving you for an inheritance to possess, you shall blot out the memory of Amalek from under heaven; you shall not forget.

_____
_____
_____
_____
_____

> **Read Judges 6:1–6:**
>
> Midian Oppresses Israel
> **6** The people of Israel did what was evil in the sight of the Lord, and the Lord gave them into the hand of Midian seven years. [2] And the hand of Midian overpowered Israel, and because of Midian the people of Israel made for themselves the dens that are in the mountains and the caves and the strongholds. [3] For whenever the Israelites planted crops, the Midianites and the Amalekites and the people of the East would come up against them. [4] They would encamp against them and devour the produce of the land, as far as Gaza, and leave no sustenance in Israel and no sheep or ox or donkey. [5] For they would come up with their livestock and their tents; they would come like locusts in number—both they and their camels could not be counted—so that they laid waste the land as they came in. [6] And Israel was brought very low because of Midian. And the people of Israel cried out for help to the Lord.

LESSON 5:
HOW WE LIFE IN THE SPIRIT AND EXPERIENCE GOD'S POWER OVER THE FLESH AND THE ENEMY

This is kill, steal, and destroy. Who's really doing this? Satan. The nature of Satan, as stated in John 10:10, says the thief has come to steal, kill, and destroy. Is it periodic? Is it every now and then? No, it's constant, and it's persistent. Jesus is saying to believers: The thief who still exists and has authority over the world is coming against you to steal, kill, and destroy. It's relentless. It never stops. This is significant for our battle of the flesh versus the Spirit. Where is Satan defeated? In the Kingdom. When you're in the Spirit, he has no power over you, as he does when we are in the flesh.

If that's so and Satan knows that, what is his goal toward you? Getting you to his home turf, which is out of the Kingdom, and have you act in the flesh. God doesn't just protect you because you are a believer. Satan's defeated in the Kingdom, in the spiritual realm, which is His Kingdom. You have to be with Him in the Kingdom, which is always your choice. God says, as we have reviewed before, "I set before you life or death, blessing or cursing. If you operate in the flesh, you are walking away from the defeat that's already happened - Satan still exists and is powerful in the world, actually way more powerful than you." If God protected us regardless of our choice (walking with Him in the Spirit, or walking in the self, the flesh), He then would allow us to be acting as God, and asking Him to take care of us as we so desired in the flesh (selfishness and not following Him as King of the Kingdom). We would be demanding and would expect God to do what we want versus following Him into His perfect will, where there is protection and grandeur in His Kingdom. We are always invited to be with Him, in His place where it is the best and none better, and includes protection from Satan's persistence to steal, kill, and destroy.

> **Read Ephesians 6:10–13:**
>
> The Whole Armor of God
> [10] Finally, be strong in the Lord and in the strength of his might. [11] Put on the whole armor of God, that you may be able to stand against the schemes of the devil. [12] For we do not wrestle against flesh and blood, but against the rulers, against the authorities, against the cosmic powers over this present darkness, against the spiritual forces of evil in the heavenly places. [13] Therefore take up the whole armor of God, that you may be able to withstand in the evil day, and having done all, to stand firm.

LESSON 5:
HOW WE LIFE IN THE SPIRIT AND EXPERIENCE GOD'S POWER OVER THE FLESH AND THE ENEMY

___
___
___
___
___

You're not wrestling against flesh and blood, you're actually wrestling against the enemy, and he's got schemes, wiles, and strategies all aimed at us. Remember he's not God, so he's not omnipresent, not omnipotent, not omniscient. What is he doing? He's observing you; he knows what buttons to push. What is he observing? He is observing what causes you to go to the flesh. He then works to create the cause to have you either exit the Kingdom (go from the Spirit/Kingdom to the flesh) or stay in the flesh and not go back to following God. He then sits back and watches us self–destruct.

> **Read 1 Peter 5:8:**
>
> [8] Be sober-minded; be watchful. Your adversary the devil prowls around like a roaring lion, seeking someone to devour.

___
___
___
___
___

Satan is like a lion, prowling around, looking for someone to devour. What does a lion do? It prowls around, observing, and then attacking the weak link. The lion discovers who the weakest link is and then goes after it to devour it. When is he doing that? All the time. As king of the jungle, he can. What is he looking at in your life? Your weaknesses. He will go after your weak spots in the flesh, and then steal, kill, and destroy your life using those weaknesses.

LESSON 5:
HOW WE LIFE IN THE SPIRIT AND EXPERIENCE GOD'S POWER OVER THE FLESH AND THE ENEMY

> **Read James 1:12–18:**
>
> [12] Blessed is the man who remains steadfast under trial, for when he has stood the test he will receive the crown of life, which God has promised to those who love him. [13] Let no one say when he is tempted, "I am being tempted by God," for God cannot be tempted with evil, and he himself tempts no one. [14] But each person is tempted when he is lured and enticed by his own desire. [15] Then desire when it has conceived gives birth to sin, and sin when it is fully grown brings forth death.
>
> [16] Do not be deceived, my beloved brothers. [17] Every good gift and every perfect gift is from above, coming down from the Father of lights, with whom there is no variation or shadow due to change.[a] [18] Of his own will he brought us forth by the word of truth, that we should be a kind of firstfruits of his creatures.

_____
_____
_____
_____
_____

    As we understood from James 1:2, if it's a trial from God, it is a test of what? Faith. This means we have been given a word, a promise, an instruction that He has spoken to us personally, and then asks us to follow Him by faith (which He then tests by bringing a trial to see if we believe, have faith, and are willing to completely follow). God says, "There is going to be a trial that comes from the enemy, don't ever attribute that to Me. I am not tempting you to draw you into temptation." Think about the battle of the Spirit and the flesh: What is temptation to the flesh? God wants you to stay in the Spirit, in the Kingdom, but Satan is working to lure you and entice you by your own desires (the flesh). He appeals to something that you find desirable in the flesh. And when you exit the Kingdom and go to the flesh, it then becomes sin (not walking with God but seeking your own way).

LESSON 5:
HOW WE LIFE IN THE SPIRIT AND EXPERIENCE GOD'S POWER OVER THE FLESH AND THE ENEMY

> **Read James 4:1–6:**
>
> Warning Against Worldliness
> **4** What causes quarrels and what causes fights among you? Is it not this, that your passions[a] are at war within you?[b] 2 You desire and do not have, so you murder. You covet and cannot obtain, so you fight and quarrel. You do not have, because you do not ask. 3 You ask and do not receive, because you ask wrongly, to spend it on your passions. 4 You adulterous people![c] Do you not know that friendship with the world is enmity with God? Therefore, whoever wishes to be a friend of the world makes himself an enemy of God. 5 Or do you suppose it is to no purpose that the Scripture says, "He yearns jealously over the spirit that he has made to dwell in us"? 6 But he gives more grace. Therefore, it says, "God opposes the proud but gives grace to the humble.

_____
_____
_____
_____
_____

Friendship with the world (self) is what? Enmity against God. Why? Because you're not asking God, you are in the flesh, you're not even caring. No wonder you have all kinds of problems. Or maybe you asked God, but you have a miss. In other words, you missed the mark, you missed His process. He has a way He'd like you to do things, how He'd like you to do them, and you missed it.

We have the privilege of seeking and receiving His will.

> **Read Ephesians 6:13–20:**
>
> 13 Therefore take up the whole armor of God, that you may be able to withstand in the evil day, and having done all, to stand firm. 14 Stand therefore, having fastened on the belt of truth, and having put on the breastplate of righteousness, 15 and, as shoes for your feet, having put on the readiness given by the gospel of peace. 16 In all circumstances take up the shield of faith, with which you can extinguish all the flaming darts of the evil one; 17 and take the helmet of salvation, and the sword of the Spirit, which is the word of God, 18 praying at all

LESSON 5:
HOW WE LIFE IN THE SPIRIT AND EXPERIENCE GOD'S POWER OVER THE FLESH AND THE ENEMY

> times in the Spirit, with all prayer and supplication. To that end, keep alert with all perseverance, making supplication for all the saints, [19] and also for me, that words may be given to me in opening my mouth boldly to proclaim the mystery of the gospel, [20] for which I am an ambassador in chains, that I may declare it boldly, as I ought to speak.

_____

_____

_____

_____

If you're going to overcome the attack, the wiles, the schemes of the enemy (to appeal to self and draw you away from the Kingdom of God, from God's will), you've got to put on the armor of God. By putting on the armor of God, where are you? Living in the Spirit, in the Kingdom. That's only where protection and overcoming happens. And He says: stand, stand, stand. In other words, stay in the Kingdom. Stay in the Spirit. Don't exit. Don't try to do this on your own. Stand here and let Him fulfill His wonderful will and protection of it by these processes:

1. Put on the belt of truth. Go to the truth. What's the truth? What's really happening here? See what Satan's up to. See his process. See the situation and understand it.

2. Put on the breastplate of righteousness. Who is righteousness? Christ. Stay with Him. He's going to give you the protection that you need. Why? Christ has already defeated him. Satan can't get to you. Stay with Christ!

3. Put peace on your feet. What do you do with your feet? Go into battle and march forward. He said: Before you do, make sure you're in the Kingdom, with the Spirit of shalom, peace. Are you agitated, upset, anxious, worried? If so, you're in the flesh, and you're going to lose this battle. So, this gives you an indicator: If you're going to go to battle, are you at peace in yourself? Because the Kingdom of God (Romans 14:17) is righteousness, peace, and joy in the Holy Spirit.

LESSON 5:
HOW WE LIFE IN THE SPIRIT AND EXPERIENCE GOD'S POWER OVER THE FLESH AND THE ENEMY

4. Put on the shield of faith. It will extinguish anything the enemy is going to throw at you. Believe that God will shield you, and do not try to shield yourself.

5. Put on the helmet of salvation. He will have you protected with His wholeness, His deliverance, His supernatural; live there and expect His full salvation.

6. Then, with all these defensive weapons, take the offense; take up and wield the sword of the Word and receive God's answer, His promise, and pray this against the enemy, who has to flee and cannot stay in attack mode. He must retreat as you go after him (who has already been defeated) with the sword, God's Word.

Read through these sets of verses and write out the keys to overcoming the life of the flesh (self) and living in the Spirit. What is the role of the Holy Spirit? Why is this so significant to us enjoying life and receiving all that God wants to deliver to us for our Covenant experience in our everyday lives?

> **Read Matthew 16:24–27:**
>
> Take Up Your Cross and Follow Jesus
> [24] Then Jesus told his disciples, "If anyone would come after me, let him deny himself and take up his cross and follow me. [25] For whoever would save his life[a] will lose it, but whoever loses his life for my sake will find it. [26] For what will it profit a man if he gains the whole world and forfeits his soul? Or what shall a man give in return for his soul? [27] For the Son of Man is going to come with his angels in the glory of his Father, and then he will repay each person according to what he has done.

_____
_____
_____
_____
_____

He says: the key again is to stay in the Kingdom, stay in the Spirit where the power is. The first thing you've got to do is what? Deny self. You've got to go through Gethsemane and say that you truly surrender your will to His, instead of deciding on your own what you want to do. You need to seek Him, seek His will,

LESSON 5:
HOW WE LIFE IN THE SPIRIT AND EXPERIENCE GOD'S POWER OVER THE FLESH AND THE ENEMY

and deny self. Then, take up the cross. Stand on what Christ has already done. You don't have to go through it. He's done it for you. What did He do with the cross? He provided the way to relationship with Him and gained victory over the enemy, who has no power over us in His Kingdom.

God has given you life—abundant life; and He's given you the ability to follow Him. Stand on that. Deny self, go to the cross, and put to death the flesh. Once that is done, you are in a position to do what? Follow Him. All the power is now available to you in the spiritual place. So, to follow Him into His will, best and none better, you are to: surrender your will because you believe that God's will is best and none better. Put to death the flesh. Stand on the victory of the cross, and then follow Christ who will lead you, guide you and show you His will.

> **Read Romans 8:12–17:**
>
> Heirs with Christ
> [12] So then, brothers,[a] we are debtors, not to the flesh, to live according to the flesh. [13] For if you live according to the flesh you will die, but if by the Spirit you put to death the deeds of the body, you will live. [14] For all who are led by the Spirit of God are sons[b] of God. [15] For you did not receive the spirit of slavery to fall back into fear, but you have received the Spirit of adoption as sons, by whom we cry, "Abba! Father!" [16] The Spirit himself bears witness with our spirit that we are children of God, [17] and if children, then heirs—heirs of God and fellow heirs with Christ, provided we suffer with him in order that we may also be glorified with him.

_____
_____
_____
_____
_____

LESSON 5:
HOW WE LIFE IN THE SPIRIT AND EXPERIENCE GOD'S POWER OVER THE FLESH AND THE ENEMY

Paul, in Romans 7, says the default is going back to the flesh, but here he says do not accept this as your obligation, or normal. You don't have to stay there. You're not obligated to or indebted to the flesh, but rather, as a child of God, you are to be what? (Romans 7:14) Led by the Spirit. His role is to lead you and your role is to follow Him, living the life of a toddler. "Abba, Father. I'll go with you today, with great enthusiasm, joy, and expectation. I'll go where You lead me." And, as you're a child of God, He will confirm (Romans 7:16) that you're His child. He's going to lead you. We can go to Abba Daddy at any time and have a conversation to understand how to follow Him. Continue to be led by the Spirit, which is actually our privilege and our identity.

> **Read John 16:13–15:**
>
> [13] When the Spirit of truth comes, he will guide you into all the truth, for he will not speak on his own authority, but whatever he hears he will speak, and he will declare to you the things that are to come. [14] He will glorify me, for he will take what is mine and declare it to you. [15] All that the Father has is mine; therefore, I said that he will take what is mine and declare it to you.

_____
_____
_____
_____
_____

The Spirit of truth will guide you into all truth. This is everything that's going on in a situation, including all the spiritual dimensions, your heart, and understanding what is really happening. What is the truth? Come with Him and follow Him into the truth. He'll tell you of things to come. He'll alert you. Follow Him. If you can't figure it out yet, let Him deliver to you what He has in mind and in His timing. He will guide you into all truth, so pay attention. Let's go.

LESSON 5:
HOW WE LIFE IN THE SPIRIT AND EXPERIENCE GOD'S POWER OVER THE FLESH AND THE ENEMY

> **Read Matthew 18:18–20:**
>
> [18] Truly, I say to you, whatever you bind on earth shall be bound in heaven, and whatever you loose on earth shall be loosed[a] in heaven. [19] Again I say to you, if two of you agree on earth about anything they ask, it will be done for them by my Father in heaven. [20] For where two or three are gathered in my name, there am I among them."

_____

_____

_____

_____

_____

If you gather in My name, what are you doing? You're seeking My will. You do this in community—with your spouse, your family, your friends, your inner circle, your small group. You seek confirmation about what the group is hearing regarding receiving God's will. You stay with this gathering in His name until you reach unity of the Spirit, agreement on what is God's will. He says: When you get to unity, you now know with certainty and clarity His will, and now you can pray that with great confidence. The Father will deliver what He has now shown you through community, through confirmation of unity of receiving His will. You now have power over the principalities because you can bind them up from attack (as discussed previously) and you can loose all the power of heaven. The Spirit will get us there. One hundred percent of the time.

So, as we end this study, consider the following summary.

Read through these verses and write out the summary of all the keys to enjoying life in the Spirit. How, then, are we to adjust our lives to walking in the Spirit every day and enjoying the benefits of life in the Spirit?

> **Read Psalm 24:1–10:**
>
> The King of Glory
> A Psalm of David.
> **24** The earth is the Lord's and the fullness thereof,[a]
>   the world and those who dwell therein,

LESSON 5:
HOW WE LIFE IN THE SPIRIT AND EXPERIENCE GOD'S POWER OVER THE FLESH AND THE ENEMY

> 2 for he has founded it upon the seas
>   and established it upon the rivers.
> 3 Who shall ascend the hill of the Lord?
>   And who shall stand in his holy place?
> 4 He who has clean hands and a pure heart,
>   who does not lift up his soul to what is false
>   and does not swear deceitfully.
> 5 He will receive blessing from the Lord
>   and righteousness from the God of his salvation.
> 6 Such is the generation of those who seek him,
>   who seek the face of the God of Jacob.[b] Selah
> 7 Lift up your heads, O gates!
>   And be lifted up, O ancient doors,
>   that the King of glory may come in.
> 8 Who is this King of glory?
>   The Lord, strong and mighty,
>   the Lord, mighty in battle!
> 9 Lift up your heads, O gates!
>   And lift them up, O ancient doors,
>   that the King of glory may come in.
> 10 Who is this King of glory?
>   The Lord of hosts,
>   he is the King of glory! Selah

_____
_____
_____
_____
_____

Recognize these verses? The stanzas of the Messiah by Handel (usually sung at Easter); seek the God of Jacob. He took everything that we've just processed and said, "You know what Jacob went through, right?" Though he had issues of the flesh, he did have a heart to follow God. It was a struggle, but, through the wrestling, he surrendered and was blessed. Who can ascend to the Holy Hill? The one who's blameless. Christ, in His Kingdom, living in the Spirit and not the flesh. Seek the God of Jacob and He will bless you. He has power over your

LESSON 5:
HOW WE LIFE IN THE SPIRIT AND EXPERIENCE GOD'S POWER OVER THE FLESH AND THE ENEMY

circumstances, over everything that He created. He is superior. He can make it happen. He says, "Seek Me, stay with Me, and walk with Me." He wants you to learn everything about Jacob, and to live that way. "Learn that way and stay with Me, and I will come." Where? Into your life, into any situation. "I can handle this, I can take care of this, I can resolve it."

So, it's a choice—either live in the flesh where there will be struggle, you will be attacked, and you will not enjoy the fullness of life, or live in the Spirit and receive the blessing, the abundant life, full protection, and the righteousness, peace, and joy of the Kingdom, all which come through the Spirit.

www.ingramcontent.com/pod-product-compliance
Lightning Source LLC
LaVergne TN
LVHW071657060526
838201LV00037B/369